# Praise for Seattle Justice

"*Seattle Justice* provides a colorful, fascinating portrait of the ugly underbelly of the city and reveals how a well-intentioned tolerance policy undermines the morality of law enforcement institutions and leads to pervasive crime."

—SAM REED, Washington secretary of state, 2001 to 2013

"As candidate and prosecutor, Bayley led the cleanup of Seattle corruption. That he and his team did it largely through the political system shows the reforming power of representative democracy. There is a lesson here for right now in America. Sovereignty resides with the people, after all."

—BRUCE CHAPMAN, Seattle city councilmember, 1971 to 1975, founder of Discovery Institute

"This is a well-documented and lively story that is part youth movement, part political movement, and all about a properly aroused band of citizens focused on changing their city for the better. And, ultimately, doing it."

—CHARLEY ROYER, former Seattle mayor

"*Seattle Justice* tells firsthand the important story of how a few dedicated reformers changed a corrupt civic culture. The battle was as much against complacency as the wrongdoing itself. Every generation needs its Bayleys to challenge the indifference and inertia of its time."

—TED VAN DYK, author of *Heroes, Hacks, and Fools* and longtime Democratic national policy advisor

"I am not a fan of detective stories or police procedurals, and have never lived in Seattle (worse, I'm a 49ers fan). But I was drawn into *Seattle Justice*. Bayley writes crisply and clearly, sorting out the characters and transforming this tangled web into a fascinating tale of municipal corruption and cleanup."

—JOHN ROCKWELL, former *New York Times* arts critic

# *SEATTLE JUSTICE*

★ ★ ★ ★ ★ ★ ★ ★ ★ ★ ★ ★

## THE RISE AND FALL of the POLICE PAYOFF SYSTEM IN SEATTLE

★ ★ ★ ★ ★ ★ ★ ★ ★ ★ ★ ★

## CHRISTOPHER T. BAYLEY

SASQUATCH BOOKS
SEATTLE

# For Cynthia, Elizabeth, and Kate

Printed in the United States of America
Published by Sasquatch Books
19 18 17 16 15     9 8 7 6 5 4 3 2 1

Editor: Hannah Elnan
Production editor: Em Gale
Author's assistant: Glenn MacGilvra
Cover design: Mikko Kim
Interior design: Anna Goldstein
Copyeditor: Janice Lee

Library of Congress Cataloging-in-Publication Data is available.
ISBN: 978-1-63217-029-3
Sasquatch Books
1904 Third Avenue, Suite 710
Seattle, WA 98101
(206) 467-4300
www.sasquatchbooks.com
custserv@sasquatchbooks.com

### PHOTO CREDITS

COVER: *(right)* Christopher T. Bayley by Mary Randlett; *(left)* Charles O. Carroll,
courtesy of King County Archives (John Spellman presenting a silver engraved
tray to Charles O. Carroll, January 7, 1971. King County Executive John Spellman
photograph files, Series 413, Box 1, Item 92.0.0140. King County Archives)
PAGES 78 AND 137: Courtesy of the Post-Intelligencer
PAGE 80: Courtesy of Gannett
PAGE 95: Courtesy of KCPA files
PAGES 97, 98, 103, 124, 126, 131, 188, AND 190: Courtesy of Post-Intelligencer
Collection, Museum of History and Modern Industry

# CONTENTS

★ ★ ★ ★ ★ ★ ★ ★ ★ ★ ★ ★

# CAST OF CHARACTERS

★ ★ ★ ★ ★ ★ ★ ★ ★ ★ ★ ★

**ACTION FOR WASHINGTON (AFW):** Youth organization founded in 1968 to support statewide Republican ticket

**AIKEN, PATRICIA "PAT" HARBER:** King County deputy prosecutor under Charles O. Carroll, assistant chief criminal deputy under Christopher T. Bayley

**AKERS, GEORGE:** In charge of 1970 campaign finances

**ALBERG, TOM:** Member of CHECC and Ripon Society, chair of 1970 campaign

**ALLISON, RICHARD:** 1970 campaign manager, chief of staff in prosecutor's office under Christopher Bayley

**ANDERSON, GENE:** Chief deputy of the fraud division, created in 1971

**BAILEY, PHILIP W. "PHIL":** Publisher of Seattle weekly newspaper the *Argus*

**BERGER, CHARLES "CHARLIE":** Proprietor of Lifeline Club bingo parlor

**BLUE—RIBBON COMMITTEE:** Three citizens appointed by Mayor Braman in 1967 to investigate reports of police corruption

**BOEING, WILLIAM "BILL", JR.:** Business leader and financial supporter of Charles O. Carroll

**BOERNER, DAVID "DAVE":** Washington assistant attorney general under John O'Connell, later chief criminal deputy under Christopher Bayley

**BRAMAN, DORM:** Three-term councilmember and Seattle mayor, 1964–69

**BRUCE, REG:** Investigator for attorney general's office

**CARLSON, EDWARD E. "EDDIE":** Business leader, Seattle World's Fair founder, organized business support for Bayley in 1970 general election

**CARROLL, CHARLES M. "STREETCAR CHARLIE":** Seattle city councilmember, 1950–72

**CARROLL, CHARLES O. "CHUCK":** King County prosecutor, 1948–70

**CHAMBLISS, WILLIAM J.:** UW sociologist, author of *On the Take: From Petty Crooks to Presidents*

**CHAPMAN, BRUCE K.:** Member of CHECC and Ripon Society, Seattle city councilmember from 1971 until appointed Washington secretary of state, 1975–1980

**CHECC:** Choose an Effective City Council, founded 1967 to promote reform city council candidates

**CICHY, BEN:** Public representative of Farwest Novelty Company, holder of King County's only pinball license; found drowned near his waterfront home in May 1969

**CLARK, RON:** King County deputy prosecutor under Carroll and Bayley

**CLINTON, GORDON:** Seattle mayor, 1956–64

**COLACURCIO, FRANK:** Owner of strip clubs, indicted with Charles Berger by Stan Pitkin

**COLE, WILLIAM:** Superior court judge visiting from Kittitas County who made key rulings in conspiracy case

**CONSIDINE, JOHN:** Turn-of-the-century theatrical impresario, proprietor of box houses and winner of a gunfight

**COOK, M. E. "BUZZ":** Seattle assistant police chief, indicted by federal grand jury and convicted of perjury in 1970

**CORR, EUGENE:** Seattle assistant police chief, part of Palace Guard, forced out of office

**CUNNINGHAM, ROSS:** *Seattle Times* chief political editor

**DAVIDSON, BOB:** AFW intern, 1970 deputy campaign manager

**DENNY, VICTOR:** Descendant of one of Seattle's founders, financial supporter of Charles O. Carroll

**DEVIN, WILLIAM F.:** Seattle mayor, 1942–52

**DYSART, KEITH:** 1970 campaign team; planned Lake City Ambush

**EVANS, DANIEL J. "DAN":** Washington governor, 1965–77

**FRAYN, MORT:** Seattle establishmentarian, 1969 mayoral candidate

**GAIN, CHARLES:** Acting Seattle police chief, July–August 1970

**GILL, HIRAM:** Elected Seattle's mayor in 1910, recalled in 1911, served again 1914–18

**GORTON, SLADE:** Washington attorney general, 1968–81

**GUSTIN, ANTON "TONY":** Seattle assistant police chief, instigator of the Lifeline Club raid

**GUZZO, LOU:** *Seattle Post-Intelligencer* managing editor, 1960s

**HAGA, ERIC:** Cold case of his wife and daughter's 1966 murder reopened in 1971, convicted of murder in 1971, finally confirmed after appeals in 1975

**HALL, CAMDEN "CAM":** Coleader of Initiative 229 campaign, cochair of CHECC and member of 1970 campaign team

**HAUBERG, JOHN:** Arts and business leader, funder of AFW and 1970 campaign

**HEAVEY, ED:** Candidate for King County prosecutor in 1970 and 1974

**HOWELL, LEMBHARD "LEM":** Coleader of Initiative 229 campaign, civil rights attorney, candidate for prosecutor in 1970

**JACKSON, HENRY M. "SCOOP":** Washington's junior senator, 1960s

**JESSUP, DAVID:** SPD officer who attempted independent investigation of payoffs

**LANDES, BERTHA:** Seattle mayor, 1926–28, a reformer and Seattle's only female mayor

**LARKIN, WAYNE:** SPD officer, president of Seattle Police Officers' Guild, Seattle city councilmember 1969–77

**LEAGUE OF WOMEN VOTERS:** Led city charter reform efforts in 1960s

**MAGNANO, MARCO:** King County deputy prosecutor under both Carroll and Bayley

**MAGNUSON, WARREN G. "MAGGIE":** Washington's senior senator, 1960s and 1970s

**MALENG, NORM:** Chief civil deputy and leader of conspiracy trial team, elected King County prosecutor in 1978

**MCBROOM, RICHARD "DICK":** Chief of 1971 King County grand jury staff

**MEYERS, VIC:** Washington secretary of state, 1956–64, in office at time of the Great Referendum Robbery

**MIFFLIN, JAMES W.:** King County Superior Court judge who presided over conspiracy trial

**MONSON, KEN, AND H. N. TIBBETTS:** Funder and fund conduit for puppet ad in last days of 1970 final election

**MOORE, FRANK:** Acting Seattle police chief, 1969–70

**MUNICIPAL LEAGUE OF KING COUNTY:** Civic organization that rates candidates for local office

**NEW ORDER OF CINCINNATUS:** Group of young Seattle political reformers in the mid-1930s

**O'CONNELL, JOHN J.:** Washington attorney general, 1956–68

**PELLY, THOMAS M. "TOM":** Longtime Republican congressman, succeeded by Joel Pritchard

**PHELPS, SHEF:** Business leader and funder of AFW and 1970 campaign

**PITKIN, STAN:** US attorney, Western Washington, 1969–74

**POMEROY, ALLAN:** Seattle mayor, 1952–56

**PRITCHARD, JOEL:** State legislator, member of Congress, Washington lieutenant governor

**RAHR, SUE:** Former King County sheriff, currently a leader in officer training

**RAMON, FRANK:** Seattle police chief, 1960–69, who resigned after Palace Revolt in 1969

**REESE, ROBERT:** Shot by police in 1965 after fight

**ROGSTAD, KEN:** King County GOP chair and ally of Charles O. Carroll

**SATTERBERG, DAN:** Current King County prosecutor

**SAVAGE, ANTHONY:** Defense attorney in conspiracy trial

**SPELLMAN, JOHN D.:** King County executive and later Washington governor

**TIELSCH, GEORGE:** Seattle police chief, 1970–74

**TOOTHMAN, EDWARD:** Acting Seattle police chief, August–September 1970

**UHLMAN, WES:** Seattle mayor, 1969–77

**WAPPENSTEIN, CHARLES:** Seattle police chief under Hiram Gill, later indicted and convicted for graft

**WARD, LARRY:** Shot by police in May 1970, shooting became the subject of an inquest and grand jury investigation

**WHEELER, DOUG:** Created community relations department in Bayley office

**WILLIAMS, JOHN T.:** Native American wood-carver, shot by police in 2010

**WILSON TWINS:** *Seattle Times* investigative reporters John and Marshall Wilson, not related

**YATES, LEE:** King County deputy prosecutor under Carroll and Bayley, tried Haga case

**YORK, GLENN:** Key witness in conspiracy trial of 1973

# INDICTMENT DAY— JULY 27, 1971

★ ★ ★ ★ ★ ★ ★ ★ ★ ★ ★ ★

It was a sunny day in July, and Seattle perched on a gray-green sound edged by mountains: the Cascades formed a wall on the east, the Olympics rose and fell across the west. I was six months into my first term as King County's prosecuting attorney, and that afternoon as the sun began to set, I sat at a big table on the fifth floor of the old King County Courthouse with the senior prosecutors who were my advisers. In front of us was an indictment, a true bill just voted on by a county grand jury. Within a few hours we would make it public.

The King County Courthouse was built in 1916 near Pioneer Square, Seattle's historic center. The Courthouse is a pile of gray stone and concrete with long marble halls where hard-soled shoes echo loudly. On the south side of the building is a small park, a place for lunch if one doesn't mind the homeless and drunks. Among them you can find a stone monument with an embedded cannonball, commemorating the day in 1856 when thousands of Native Americans attacked from thick forests surrounding the settlement, only to be discouraged by a sloop in Puget Sound firing round shot into the trees.

My office was on a corner of the fifth floor. The walls were light blue because TV cameramen preferred that as background, but the room still included a long red leather couch that had been there since Warren G. Magnuson—who by 1971 was Washington's very senior senator—was himself a young county prosecutor. Behind a sliding panel was a large conference room with a heavy oak table that filled most of the space.

A little more than a year earlier, I had stood at the end of that table as my predecessor in office, Charles O. Carroll (known as Chuck), sat at the head. On the other side was Bill Boeing Jr., son of Seattle's world famous industrialist, and Victor Denny, grandson of one of Seattle's founders, both part of Seattle's Establishment and Carroll's political allies. When we confronted each other, Carroll had been prosecutor for twenty-two years and ruled the county's Republican Party. Carroll dominated that old gray courthouse and the politicians within.

On that day in 1970, I had come there to tell Carroll that I intended to challenge him in the Republican primary. He told me I was completely unqualified. In 1971, I not only dethroned him but called a grand jury to investigate him and many others on charges of criminal conspiracy.

All that July day, the grand jury had been in session, and sitting before me and my staff was the result of their work, a multipage indictment. Our copying machine was kept busy spewing forth copies for the many people—reporters, politicians, and members of the general public—who would be interested. I asked my assistant to get the mayor of Seattle, the recently elected Wes Uhlman, on the phone. He was a Democrat; I was a Republican. I had compelled him to testify before the grand jury in previous weeks, and he had been publicly unhappy about it. It was time to give him a heads-up before releasing the indictment to the press.

When Wes was on the line, I told him the name at the top of the indictment—Carroll.

Wes interrupted. Did I mean Charlie M. "Streetcar Charlie" Carroll, a Seattle city councilmember of nearly twenty-five years? Or Chuck Carroll, the legendary King of the Courthouse?

"Both of them," I replied.

Sharing space with the Carrolls on the indictment were others: the head of King County's licensing department, responsible for gambling licenses; a former sheriff; a former police chief; an assistant police chief; and thirteen other lower-ranking police officers and sheriff's deputies. Chuck Carroll was now a criminal target along with rest, the end result of four years of stories by crusading reporters, raids by idealistic police officers, and grand juries and sensational federal trials. The bill on my conference room table charged its targets with having conducted a decades-long conspiracy to maintain a payoff system and to protect illegal gambling in return for campaign contributions. The bill indicted them and the political culture they represented, which had weathered the storms of all previous scandals and investigations for more than a hundred years. The indictment was a hinge point in Seattle's history.

Today, Seattle takes pride in being a place of clean but boring government, one operating by fair and open, albeit laborious, process. But we were not always this way. For most of Seattle's history, large chunks of the city's and county's government operations, most persistently their police departments, were corrupt. The reform of the city's political culture took place later than most people realize and required the bravery and perseverance of many people besides me.

My election in 1970 was a part of the change. I owed it to youthful pluck and fortuitous circumstances. I was part of a group of political reformers, all in our early thirties, half the age of Chuck Carroll and other leaders of the Seattle Establishment. We were Republican for the most part but had worked with Democrats to end Washington's blue laws, which forbade Sunday drinking, and to reform the Seattle City Council. Our hero and mentor was

Governor Dan Evans, who had led a statewide Republican revolution of reform politics, which we hoped to extend to Seattle.

In the office that sunny day, it all seemed inevitable—that a modern world, which had been knocking on Seattle's door, was finally there. My staff and I were young, one or two sporting mustaches and long sideburns, all of us idealists, few of us with long government experience. We welcomed the hubbub of gathered journalists and knew this was a historic day.

In the years that followed, the inevitable disappointments, the law's delays, and the difficulties of actually doing justice all knocked some of the idealism off. But I don't think our optimism was misplaced. Replacing Carroll changed Seattle for the better, and the indictment filed that day was visible proof that a change was taking place.

This book is dedicated to those who fought to make Seattle a place of honest government. They include journalists, police officers, bar owners, professors, politicians, ordinary citizens, and even a few prosecutors. Some are old now; many are gone. Their story is one worth remembering, an example of how a city can become comfortable in corruption and then will itself to do better. It is a story of how a city can reexamine the way it operates and fight to improve itself.

This is, I think, one of the important stories of Seattle, a city I have always loved and that I have always been proud to call home.

# CHAPTER 1

# OPEN CITY

★ ★ ★ ★ ★ ★ ★ ★ ★ ★ ★ ★

## City of Fortune and Vice

Seattle started profiting from vice soon after its founding. And nearly from the beginning, Seattle's city officials and law enforcement officers took their share.

In November 1851, twenty-two bedraggled pioneers from Illinois, the Denny Party, disembarked on rainy Alki Beach. Essentially, they were real estate speculators. The early pioneers, by luck and foresight, had found a favorable central location on Puget Sound, accessible by road to populated areas to the east and south, possessed of a good deep harbor, and proximate to thick forests and coal seams. They hoped their new town would attract some sort of commercial enterprise, numerous residents would arrive and prosper, and the early settlers could then sell their land claims for a profit. The gamble paid off. Forty years later, by the 1890 census, Seattle was the largest city in the new state of Washington, its 42,837 residents just edging out Tacoma's 36,006.

The city's early economic props were resource extraction: logging, coal mining, and fishing. But there were other ambitious timber and coal towns on Puget Sound. What set Seattle apart was its role as the central commercial city of the Pacific Northwest. It became the hub for numerous small passenger and freight ships known as the Mosquito Fleet. It had general stores, banks, and even a state university. In the summer, thousands of workers stopped here on their way to jobs in the woods or out at sea, and they returned to Seattle when they were laid off from fishing or lumbering in the winter. Richer men came to hire the workers, buy supplies, borrow money, make deals, or settle down with their families. These early settlers—prosperous or poor, mostly single, mostly men—didn't just want shelter, supplies, and real estate. They also wanted entertainment. Seattle became well known, on Puget Sound and later the whole West Coast, for the quality, quantity, and variety of its vice.

In 1861, John Pinnell started the Illahee, a brothel on the mudflats of Seattle, staffed by local Indian women. Before then prostitution on Puget Sound had been more casual, often transacted on boats briefly visiting logging encampments. Pinnell's brothel was a fixed attraction and highly successful. It became a civic resource and, within a few years, paid the city $1,200 each year in license fees. In fact, the Illahee may have been vital to keeping Seattle financially afloat during the dark days in the 1870s and 1880s when Seattle battled for an intercontinental railroad connection with the Northern Pacific Railway and its pet project, the city of Tacoma. According to the ever-entertaining popular historian Bill Speidel's book *Sons of the Profits*, Northern Pacific kicked Pinnell and one of his subsidiary brothels out of Tacoma following an otherwise ordinary brawl and homicide. Undeterred, Pinnell retaliated by recruiting white women from San Francisco for his Seattle brothel, keeping it the preferred destination for Puget Sound's lonely men and encouraging those traveling to Tacoma by rail to keep on heading north.

Pinnell's success attracted competitors to the area south of Pioneer Square, and soon Seattle's vice district (variously known as the Lava Beds, Skid Road, and the Tenderloin) vied for infamy with San Francisco's Barbary Coast. Seattle pioneered a new type of vice, the notorious box house. An auditorium and stage would be ringed around with second-level rooms, each with a door to a corridor, a window toward the stage, and a sofa. The women who performed on stage would often also circulate in the corridors, serving drinks and servicing customers.

Beyond serving as a commercial attraction, vice also proved to be the financial mainstay of the early city government. Although brothels were nominally illegal by territorial and state law, in practice the city enforced those laws only by exacting licenses and penalties, which carried the regularity and moral neutrality of taxes and did nothing to deter operation. At one point in the 1880s, 87 percent of the city's general fund came from brothels, gambling, and liquor. Early on, city officials faced the question of how much illegal activity should be tolerated in the name of business prosperity and city revenue.

Occasional early condemnations by preachers and Seattle's more moralistic founders had little initial impact. But by the 1880s and 1890s, the fight between vice and reform was a perennial election issue. Seattle's citizens regularly faced the choice of an open city or a closed one.

Many people in Seattle were religious, middle class, and increasingly alarmed at sharing a city with so much open vice. The city's founder, Arthur Denny, was himself a teetotaler. Coalitions of reformers and the religious sometimes won city elections on a platform of suppressing prostitution, gambling, and assorted ancillary evils. In 1884, the city banned street prostitution. In 1894, liquor sales were prohibited in box houses, quickly putting most out of business. But even when reformers captured city hall, reform was partial and temporary. Usually it was not long before a different mayor appeared with a more open attitude or an external event reversed any reform. In 1897, the Klondike Gold Rush confirmed the value of vice in emptying the pockets of prospective prospectors headed north and returning home. Open-town advocates regained power, and box houses and public brothels returned.

Seattle's early embrace of vice reached its apogee under its most shameless mayor—Hiram Gill. Gill was elected in 1910 on a platform of a wide-open city, enthusiastically supported by Colonel Blethen of the *Seattle Times*. Drinking, gambling, and most particularly prostitution would be tolerated in one section of the city as the price for keeping it out of others. Fans of the HBO show *The Wire* may recognize the idea; essentially Seattle south of Yesler would become one big Hamsterdam.

Gill hired as police chief one Charles Wappenstein, who had briefly been police chief in 1906 and was known to favor an open town. Wappenstein established open vice districts as promised but extended them further than discussed during the election. Enterprising businessmen made plans to open a five-hundred-bed bordello on Beacon Hill and persuaded the city council to make accommodations by moving a street right-of-way. This subsidized wonder never opened because Wappenstein's ever-expanding open city began to alarm even Gill's supporters.

The denouement came soon after the election. An outraged citizenry, led by the influential Reverend Mark Matthews of First Presbyterian Church, swiftly initiated a successful recall of Hiram Gill. An interim mayor named George Dilling was appointed, followed by the election of George Cotterill. Both of them promised reform but did not pursue it effectively. Hiram Gill then ran for election again, this time on a reform platform, pointing out that *he* was best equipped to clean up the city since he knew where it was dirty. Gill won his second term and subsequently led some showy attempts at vice crackdowns, smashing kegs of whiskey in illegal saloons and breaking up gambling devices. But Gill did little outside of these public acts of destruction, and his second coming did not seriously damage the commercial vice industry. It continued to thrive, though less openly.

All through these years, Seattle's vice business kept evolving, branching out into respectable entertainment while keeping its roots in the tawdry. In 1898, the theatrical impresario and entrepreneur John Considine decided to stay ahead of the competition by providing a better product. In his box houses, he separated the two professions of actress and prostitute, paying a higher wage to his entertainers who no longer circulated among the boxes. Considine opened several of what we might call "legitimate" theaters in Seattle and then up and down the West Coast, creating one of the early vaudeville circuits. Shortly afterward, an equally energetic entrepreneur named Alexander Pantages started his own vaudeville circuit and also pioneered the new field of movie theaters. Pantages opened the first of what was to become a chain of cinema palaces in Seattle, and from then on Seattle was widely known as a movie town.

While Seattle was riding its vice roller coaster, progressives at the state and national levels were passing well-intentioned mor als legislation that did little to solve the problems associated with vice districts but did a lot to ensure that official hypocrisy and corruption would accompany them. The 1889 state constitution banned "lotteries," a term courts later interpreted to cover any type of gambling. In 1909, the legislature passed blue laws prohibiting commercial activity on Sundays, including the sale of liquor. Soon afterward, liquor was prohibited completely, first by state law and then by federal law during World War I, and finally by the Eighteenth Amendment to the US Constitution.

The first fifty years of Seattle history, through 1919, set the pattern for the next fifty. Engrained in the city's consciousness was its identity as a port town providing both respectable entertainment and surreptitious vice for transient populations with money to spend. Although the example of Hiram Gill showed the public had no appetite for open tolerance of vice, there remained a constituency for allowing it to continue discreetly. Prohibition helped immensely, by forcing drinking into illegal channels where it could accompany gambling and prostitution, giving the world of vice another lucrative product.

## Police Take Their Share

Seattle did not start hiring a sizable police force until the 1880s, when a highly public lynching of three vagrants suspected of murder, as well as anti-Chinese immigration riots, persuaded the city council to come up with funds to hire a force of fifteen. As late as 1896, there were only forty-three officers for a population of sixty thousand. The effectiveness of even this small force was limited— police were told to patrol in groups no smaller than five or six to avoid attacks in the street. Nor did they get much respect from city government—police were paid little, expected to work seven days straight, and housed in cramped dormitories.

The police force grew in size and professionalism in the early twentieth century and at the same time demanded its own direct cut of vice profits, to supplement salaries. Direct evidence of police corruption in Seattle's early days is more the stuff of anecdotes than documented statistics, but the accumulation of incidents is telling.

In fact, one of Seattle's most dramatic moments of street violence, a burlesque version of the Gunfight at the OK Corral, arose from accusations of graft. In 1901, Seattle's police chief, William Meredith, and its most prominent theater operator, John Considine, became embroiled in a mutual exchange of calumny. Considine accused the police of taking protection money and then harassing him anyway. Meredith responded by accusing Considine of getting a young woman pregnant and arranging for an abortion. The city council held Considine's accusations to be more credible, in a report detailing monies paid to Meredith and then Detective Wappenstein.

The mayor duly informed Meredith that his resignation would be accepted. A couple of days later, ex-chief Meredith hunted Considine down on the streets of Seattle, a shotgun in his hand. Meredith finally caught up with Considine at a store in Pioneer Square and twice fired his shotgun at close range but still managed to miss. Considine proceeded to crack open Meredith's skull with a revolver, and then, while Considine's brother blocked onlookers from interfering, Considine put three bullets from his .38 into the dazed Meredith, who died on the spot. Considine's ensuing trial (and eventual acquittal) kept Seattle fascinated for weeks.

Aside from these dramatic moments, allegations that police accepted bribes were a regular part of political discourse and accompanied each election. For those advocating an open city, police graft was a point in their favor, on the theory that open tolerance eliminated the need for citizens to pay bribes, but this happy result never actually seemed to eventuate. In 1900, at a time when open-city policies held sway, one plaintive reformer noted that the consequence of the mayor openly levying tolls on gamblers and women of the town had not been to reduce police graft but to cause the police to seek money elsewhere.

Even Hiram Gill's grand experiment in creating vice districts did little more than convert previous fines and penalties to police payoffs. Following his brief tenure, the infamous Chief Wappenstein was convicted of bribery. At his trial, brothel operators testified to the price they had to pay to the Chief, who told them that since they had previously been paying ten dollars per bed (or "crib") as fines to the city each month, they should now just pay him ten dollars per crib directly.

The politicians took their own share. Historian Ralph Bushnell Potts tells the story of James T. Ronald, elected mayor in 1892, a time when "the police department of the city thought it had a vested property right in the collections from prostitutes and gamblers."

Ronald won on a reform ticket, but soon after election he was visited by a delegation of high-ranking police officers inquiring how much of a cut he wanted from the monthly payoff. When Ronald indignantly refused any money, the officers told him police graft was an effective method of controlling crime—"unofficial licensing." The mayor ordered the police out of his office, but as they left, one laid a gun on the table and noted somebody might get hurt. Mayor Ronald lasted less than a year before quitting, explaining that the job was ruining his health.

## Seattle Stagnates and Reform Fails

Seattle stagnated during the twenties and thirties. In the thirties, the population barely increased at all. During this time, reformers periodically attempted to root corruption out of the city, but their efforts were mostly unsuccessful as Seattle settled into a self-satisfied status quo.

In the early twenties, Seattle's women's clubs were a major source of political energy, spurring the election of Seattle's first and only female mayor, Bertha Landes. Landes first made a brief splash in 1924, when serving as acting mayor while Mayor Brown attended the Democratic National Convention in New York. Just prior to Mayor Brown heading east, Seattle's police chief William Severyns had unwisely opined to local journalists that there were at least a hundred corrupt officers on the force. The day she became acting mayor, Landes told Severyns to fire a hundred police officers and then fired him for refusing. Brown hastily returned from New York on the earliest train and reinstated Severyns as soon as he arrived.

Landes was elected mayor in her own right in 1926, the first woman mayor of a major American city. Although Mayor Landes had other concerns, like Seattle's failing public streetcar system and threats to the city's municipally owned utility City Light, she also made an issue of vice tolerance and police corruption. Sensing his political vulnerability, Chief Severyns, in the months leading up to the 1926 election, had attempted to save his reputation by detailing his valiant fight to clean up a corrupt department. The accounts, published monthly in the *Seattle Union Record*, are where some of the best-known stories of police brutality emerge, such as the practice of interrogating suspects by tying a weight around their neck and rowing them out into the middle of Lake Washington before beginning the questioning.

Unimpressed by his honesty, Landes fired Severyns again and encouraged his successor to dismiss crooked cops and arrest more gamblers and prostitutes. During her tenure, the federal government also prosecuted one of Washington's most notorious bootleggers, Roy Olmstead, an ex–Seattle police officer who controlled a fleet of boats running alcohol out of Canada and down Puget Sound.

Landes also moved to shut down dance halls, where working-class women supported their families by dancing and occasionally prostituting themselves to working-class men. But she relented after personal pleas from some of the women and opted instead to tolerate and regulate, hoping—as reformers often would in Seattle history—that setting clear rules on hours and conditions of operation would eliminate the need for dance halls to bribe the police to stay open.

Landes only had two years in office. Not long after her election, an opponent named Frank Edwards appeared, seemingly out of nowhere. Edwards received financial support from the police officers Landes had fired, as well as opponents of the City Light public power program. His platform was simple—he opposed "petticoat government." He refused to debate with the mayor, stating "any married man knows the danger of getting into an argument with a woman." Landes was endorsed by every newspaper in Seattle. Still, she lost.

Mayor Edwards fired Landes's police chief and hired his own. The open-city policy returned, as did police payoffs (if they had ever disappeared).

Reformers tried again in the early 1930s under the name of the New Order of Cincinnatus, a group of men all under thirty. The Order was ostensibly nonpartisan, though its membership leaned Republican. It backed reform city council candidates and managed to elect enough of them to dominate council committees for a time. One of their members, Arthur Langlie, became mayor and later governor. But as a group, their long-term political success was doomed by a failure to reach out to Democrats and unions.

The Order's high point came during city council hearings in July 1935, when reform councilmembers grilled police officials about public vice. Exhaustive testimony detailed addresses and operations of numerous gambling joints and houses of prostitution; the police chief simply denied any knowledge of such goings-on. Frustrated, Councilmember Fred Hamley ended the hearings by escorting the chief out of the Fourth Avenue entrance of the County-City Building and to a nearby gambling establishment where there was a roulette wheel next to its startled proprietor. The chief was shocked—shocked such a thing existed and took a proffered ax to the wheel. But the chief also remained in office. Three years later, a city councilmember noted sardonically that every location named in the city council hearing was still open.

# CHAPTER 2

# THE TOLERANCE POLICY

★ ★ ★ ★ ★ ★ ★ ★ ★ ★ ★ ★

### Devin Begins a New Fight

In the 1940s, a new mayor initiated a new approach, the Tolerance Policy. This regime operated nearly continuously until 1969 and represented Seattle's official compromise between the attractions of commercial vice and the obligations of official morality.

William Devin was a protégé of Mayor Langlie and was associated with the Order. Before being elected mayor in 1942, Devin had been a police-court judge, responsible for minor criminal offenses, which put him in a good position to observe both Seattle's law enforcement and law infringement communities. As judge, Devin won attention by rigorously enforcing the new system of sequentially numbering traffic tickets and keeping copies in triplicate, to make it difficult for police to fix tickets.

In the early forties, Seattle was wide open. Brothels were numerous and easy to find, as were bookmaking parlors and slot machines, though the latter were theoretically confined to private clubs. Big-money card games were common. Because of Washington's restrictive liquor laws (until an initiative was passed in 1948, public establishments could not sell liquor by the drink), there were many speakeasies years after Prohibition officially ended. The city council licensed card rooms, though ostensibly the games were for entertainment, not money—that is, rummy, not poker. Accusations were constant that the police or city officials or both were on the take.

Newly elected Mayor Devin opposed an open town but had little influence over law enforcement policy because he had little control over the police department. In 1942, the chief was Herbert Kimsey, who was guaranteed a five-year term by the city charter. Kimsey could only be removed by a two-thirds majority of city council and if there were "good cause." Ironically, this was intended to be a reform provision, created in 1934 by reformers upset at the mayor of the time, who had fired two chiefs in a dispute over how to handle a waterfront strike and eventually named himself chief. Kimsey could, and did, operate independently of the mayor. Or, sometimes, fail to operate. When the mayor complained to him about crime conditions, Kimsey usually did nothing.

Devin's chance to institute real changes came in 1943, and his leverage was World War II. Seattle was near military bases at Fort Lewis, Bremerton, and Everett, and had its own base inside city limits at Fort Lawton. By 1943, these bases were bursting with soldiers and sailors, and those returning from leave in Seattle were ever more afflicted by venereal disease. The officer in charge of Paine Field near Everett sent a letter to Mayor Devin in May 1943 threatening to put seventy-four blocks of Seattle off limits to soldiers. By then, alarm at the impact of syphilis and gonorrhea on the fighting effectiveness of troops had also spread to higher levels, and soon a federal agent came to Seattle stating that the city government might need to turn over local law enforcement to the federal government. The Seattle Police Department was in danger of being run by the FBI.

Devin used this crisis to try to force a reorganization of the police force. The federal government was interested only in closing brothels and reducing disease, but for Devin, the problem went far deeper. He asked the city council to get rid of Kimsey altogether, providing them with thirty-eight specific instances of the chief failing to follow up on complaints of criminal activity—instances going far beyond prostitution.

The demand shook Kimsey. The day Devin made his demand, Kimsey told the press he had medical issues and might retire rather than endure unfair attacks. But that evening at his home in West Seattle, Kimsey huddled with senior police officers. He emerged the next day telling the press he would not leave voluntarily. In the next few weeks, the police department staged a series of raids and crackdowns to prove they were taking the federal complaints seriously. The raids themselves raised some eyebrows, as the police trashed brothels, broke up furniture, and destroyed property.

Kimsey also instituted a dizzying series of transfers of senior police officers from one department to another, replacing the existing vice officer with a woman, Captain Irene Durham. Her promotion came as a complete surprise: "I didn't ask for the job, I wasn't even consulted about it. I was told to take it by my superior officer." The department defended itself to the press, claiming problems with venereal disease were traceable to an influx of black troops who had higher rates of the disease and infected Seattle's prostitutes.

The city council did not want to fire Kimsey. One councilmember, a former Seattle police officer, suggested that instead the city reinstate the vice districts attempted by Mayor Gill. Facing council opposition, Devin withdrew his charges, biding his time. The federal agents grumbled but did not act.

Through the rest of the war and for a couple of years after, Seattle was subject to law enforcement of sporadic severity. The police and the prosecutor managed to shut down, at least temporarily, the most notorious brothels downtown and in the Central District. Major bookmaking operations, where customers could simply slip money through windows, became less public. From time to time, the police department would also go after minor gambling, arresting people for dice games in cigar stores and for using punchboards. The police continued brutal raids on suspected brothels. On one occasion, police burst into a hotel room where a soldier was sleeping with his wife and then demanded the two produce a copy of their marriage license.

But Kimsey also maintained his freedom to not act. In January 1946, he ignored Devin's direct demand that the police shut down eight speakeasies in an area around Jackson Street that had a mostly black clientele. "Where," he asked reporters, "would Negroes go to drink? In the street?"

## Devin Gets a New Police Chief

Devin's next chance to make a change came when Kimsey's term ended in 1946. A new city charter amendment returned more control over police chief selection to the mayor: chiefs had indefinite terms and the mayor could fire a chief. But the charter also imposed new limits on mayoral power—the mayor was required to choose a new chief from the top three finalists of a competitive exam, and the city council had to approve the choice.

Kimsey did not even try to apply for chief when his term expired. The city sponsored a nationwide solicitation of candidates for his replacement and even raised the salary of chief as enticement. The exam, a mixture of oral and written work, used questions created by outsiders, including police from San Francisco and Texas, and a professor from the UW Department of Sociology. An assistant chief from Kansas City, Richard R. Foster, scored highest. Second and third were two Seattle officers—police captain H. J. Lawrence and a sergeant in the Records Department, George Eastman.

Political insiders reported the police department's highest-ranking officers, the "gold braid," did not consider either Lawrence or Eastman to be part of the club but preferred either to an outsider. Foster had the reputation of a reformer, one who helped clean up the Kansas City police department after the Pendergast Machine crumbled. For the same reasons, Devin preferred Foster and pushed hard for his appointment.

For the next month, letters and petitions poured into the council. Church groups and civic organizations like the municipal league supported the mayor. On the other side appeared hundreds of identically worded postcards opposing Foster, some with the return address of the local Teamsters Hall. Ultimately the council turned down Foster 7–2, the only reason cited being that he was from out of town. Devin settled on the dark horse, Eastman, as his choice.

## The Birth of a New Policy

At thirty-three years old, Eastman was the youngest man to serve as police chief. He had numerous problems to face following the war—traffic, for example, became deadlier as ever more cars poured into downtown streets. But Eastman and Devin focused much of their efforts on vice. Within a year of Eastman's appointment, Devin announced a new regime—the Tolerance Policy.

The police, said Devin, would enforce the law "as a reasonable man would want it enforced." The policy's fuller description came later, from Ross Cunningham, then a political reporter for the *Seattle Times* and a supporter of Devin. As Cunningham reported, the police would continue the crackdown against houses of prostitution and bookmaking establishments. And for the first time, the police would eliminate all slot machines, including those in private clubs, as well as punchboards paying in cash. However, the police would not enforce gambling laws against punchboards that paid off in merchandise or against card rooms where bets stayed for small stakes—under a dollar. All a card room operator needed to do to operate legal poker games was to get a card room license from the city council and to obey the police's informal guidelines. Devin's ultimate goal was to make the rules regarding vice enforcement so clear and so transparent that honest merchants would no longer need to bribe the police to be left alone. The Tolerance Policy was squarely directed at curbing corrupt police.

Devin also defended the policy as a major step toward eliminating vice. Only a few years before, Seattle had been wide open, but it was now committed to systematically and persistently enforcing laws against major gambling and open prostitution. Allowing minor gambling at the same time was simply a practical accommodation to reality and public opinion.

## Devin against the "Forces of Evil"

Although the Tolerance Policy effectively constituted Seattle's vice law for the next twenty-two years, it was always controversial. Initially the policy was closely identified with the Devin-Eastman administration, and those two had their enemies, both in and out of the police department.

In 1948, Devin ran for reelection against Allan Pomeroy, a former assistant US attorney. The election became a battle between those preferring the older, more open Seattle and those defending Devin's Tolerance Policy as the best weapon against major vice. Ranking officers of the police department supported Pomeroy to get rid of Eastman, who they considered a jumped-up sergeant, too inexperienced and too reformist for the taste of the old guard.

On the other hand, the church groups of Seattle were all for Devin and painted the election in near apocalyptic terms. One church leader thundered, "The Forces of Evil are now at work to get Mayor Devin out of the way so that corruption may once again find its way into Seattle." Also on Devin's side was the *Seattle Times*. Its articles and editorials contained dark warnings that slot machine lobbyists were seeking a return to their glory days by supporting Pomeroy. In the end, Devin earned a narrow victory over Pomeroy, and the Tolerance Policy gained another four years of official support.

The 1952 election was a replay—again, Devin versus Pomeroy. As far as Devin was concerned, there was still only one real issue in the campaign—whether the slot machine interests could get rid of him and Eastman and make Seattle an open town again. On the other side, much of the police department still disliked Eastman. Before the election, Eastman claimed some police were writing extra traffic tickets for the express purpose of turning voters against Devin. In his own turn, though focusing on other issues, Pomeroy criticized the Tolerance Policy as officially condoned illegality. He promised to end it and to get rid of Eastman if elected.

By a margin of victory as narrow as his previous defeat, Pomeroy was elected. Pomeroy eventually selected for chief H. J. Lawrence, who had been passed over in 1946. Between them, Pomeroy and Lawrence announced an end to the Tolerance Policy, at least as regards card rooms. No longer would poker games be allowed, even with limits as low as a dollar.

As Devin was leaving, the Tolerance Policy got its own trial, in a remarkable three-day hearing held in the old Field Artillery Armory (subsequently the Seattle Center's Food Circus and now, again, the Armory). In 1952, the state legislature's Council on Crime, headed by ambitious young senator Albert Rosellini, was touring the state to investigate local crime conditions. Seattle's turn took place in June, just after the change of mayors.

Rosellini's targets included Devin, Eastman, and the Tolerance Policy. Although the mayor's office was nominally nonpartisan, Devin was usually identified with the Republican Party. Republicans claimed the hearings were designed only to advance Rosellini's political prospects by blaming crime on the Republicans. In the hearing, Rosellini accused Devin and Eastman of being "defeatist" and "fatalistic" by condoning open gambling. Eastman admitted, "My job is to establish certain levels of enforcement even though they appear on the surface to violate the law." Four years later, Rosellini was elected governor where he served two terms.

Pomeroy was mayor from 1952 to 1956 and demonstrated that it was easier to condemn the Tolerance Policy than abandon it. Officially, he proclaimed laws against gambling would be enforced to the letter. In practice, he left this to the discretion of Chief Lawrence, a man happy to tolerate a wide range of vice. Pomeroy's ban on card room gambling, to the extent it was enforced at all, lasted approximately a year, after which stories emerged in the papers that card room operators "had been advised" by persons unidentified that gambling for money was OK again. Confronted with these reports, Lawrence stated that he would look into it. Pomeroy said little at all.

In 1956, Pomeroy faced the young and energetic Gordon Clinton, solidly backed by Seattle's Establishment. Clinton's campaign workers went out into Seattle nightlife to investigate conditions and easily found poker games in card rooms with limits from four to ten dollars. Once again vice was a mayoral campaign issue, and again the reformer won. But Clinton had made no promises regarding the Tolerance Policy. Once in power, he accepted its return as Seattle's official philosophy of vice law enforcement.

## Deeper, More Powerful Forces

As Devin struggled to assert control over Seattle's commercial vice in the '40s, his enemies were ostensibly Chief Kimsey, the city council, and Pomeroy. But another formidable and barely disguised opponent was the senior leadership of Seattle's police department and, perhaps, their friends among the gambling interests. Seattle's high-ranking officers persuaded Kimsey to resist being ousted in 1943 and lobbied their allies on the city council to keep him. In 1946, senior officials were solidly against having the outsider Foster appointed and again had the council's backing. And in 1948 and 1952, the old guard backed Pomeroy as a means of getting rid of Eastman.

In 1943, after Chief Kimsey announced he would fight to keep his job, Devin said, "[I felt] sorry for Kimsey. I am satisfied he is not doing what he would like to do. He is being influenced by other persons to make this move. . . . I feel we're fighting some far deeper, more powerful forces in this city and that the chief is simply the goat." Whether Devin meant ranking officers of the department or wealthy gambling operators or both in alliance isn't clear.

Police leadership over the years showed a remarkable solidarity—for example, when Lawrence was appointed chief in 1952. Clearly the department favorite, he was still forced by the city charter to take the same exam required of all candidates and had to place in the top three to be chosen. His scores initially placed him eighth out of seventeen applicants. The department threw out some of the essay questions, raising his rank to fifth. And at that point, three of the four applicants ahead of Lawrence, including two who would later become assistant chiefs, M. E. Cook and Al Rouse, withdrew from the competition, allowing Pomeroy to choose Lawrence. None of the top candidates were from outside Seattle's department, for Pomeroy had done little national outreach.

## Tolerating Graft

Eliminating graft was the raison d'être for the Tolerance Policy. However, Devin and Eastman achieved mixed results. Eastman may have been personally honest, but he shied from direct confrontation and filed no charges against police officers. In the fall of 1947, Eastman removed the captain in charge of regulating illegal liquor establishment because nothing was actually being done about the hundred or so speakeasies in Seattle. The officer faced no imprisonment and no disgrace, but simply reassignment. During his grilling by Rosellini at the Armory, Eastman admitted he asked the IRS to investigate some police officers to check on their sources of income, but he would not identify who and indicated he failed to follow up on the IRS investigation.

One peculiar episode illustrates Eastman's good intentions and his limitations, as well as the municipal culture of the time. Eastman fired everyone at the police garage because of their "misuse of resources," including repairing and maintaining the personal cars of city councilmembers. The councilmembers defended themselves by saying that from time to time they gave ten dollars to the police-garage mechanics' "tobacco fund" and that, by the way, Eastman and Devin were tapping their phones.

This latter charge received scant attention; an attempted investigation was quashed by other councilmembers, who ruled it was outside the jurisdiction of the city council. Remarkably, Ross Cunningham of the *Seattle Times* reported that "it was common knowledge" at the council that there were wiretaps on councilmember phones; it just wasn't known who placed them or why. As for the staff at the police garage, Eastman quickly rehired them.

Many years later, Eastman was asked if an honest, aggressive policeman could survive in a department where there was corruption. His opinion sounded like a self-assessment: "Yes, . . . he can work to retirement but he will probably lose his aggressiveness and ambition. He can EXIST indefinitely but his effectiveness will be compromised."

Devin and Eastman did probably change some of the mechanics of Seattle's police graft. Before Devin, numerous semipublic establishments, including brothels, speakeasies, and bookmakers, could be tapped on a regular basis at their fixed addresses. (In the 1940s, some police officers may have been part owners of the brothels, a bit of vertical integration that would have neatly eliminated the need for graft.) After Devin and Eastman cracked down on major vice, officially allowing only low-stakes gambling, police sought more payoffs from less obvious targets, including taverns, dance clubs, and card rooms, regardless of their immediate connection with vice. Under Chief Lawrence and his successor, Frank Ramon, the payoff system inflicted on downtown businesses became highly organized.

For Seattle's boosters, the contrast between conditions before the war and the tighter control imposed by Devin was remarkable, while the ongoing graft was invisible. A representative voice was the irrepressibly optimistic Ralph Bushnell Potts. Potts helped found the New Order of Cincinnatus but by the 1950s had mellowed into a historian of Seattle's greatness. In 1955, he concluded his history of the city with serene complacency, congratulating Devin for cleaning up a once sullied city, and banishing graft and vice to the dustbins of history:

> There wasn't in 1943 and there isn't in 1955 one house of prostitution open. There wasn't then and there isn't in 1955 a Chinese lottery or big gambling establishment running. There may be prostitutes and there may be tinhorn gamblers abroad in the city, but for once they have no police protection. . . .
>
> Perhaps the greatest wonder of all was that when it happened, nobody wondered. . . . Frankly, a great many people

never knew there was a change, and those that did had nothing to say about it. It seemed to be as immutable as the tide. It had at last gone out and carried with it the corruption of over seventy years. And there is no demand that it return.

Potts's sense of his own city was a little off, for there certainly were brothels open in 1943. But still, this passage exemplifies the optimism and delusion of Seattle's self-image in the fifties and sixties—that somehow, without anything being said, Seattle's previous years of graft and corruption had slipped out to sea with the tide.

## King County's Chief Law—Enforcement Officer

In January 1950, a small-time bookmaker was arrested in Seattle. Perhaps to switch the blame to others who the police might be more interested in, or perhaps simply because he was talkative, the bookmaker told the police he "laid off" his larger-scale bets to other bigger bookmakers—ensuring he would not be wiped out if a gambler won. Of course, this implied that in Seattle there were larger-scale bookmakers. The police relayed this information to the prosecutor, Charles O. "Chuck" Carroll. The bookie eventually pled guilty to a reduced charge of gambling and paid a $200 fine.

By July 1950, congressional hearings revealing a national syndicate of horse-race gamblers had made headlines. Carroll told the press he was launching a local investigation. His first step was to call the hapless bookie back into his office and, in the presence of the police chief and the head of the patrol division, ask him if he stood by his story that he laid off bets. No, replied the bookie; he had just made up that earlier story to get off the hook—there was nothing to it. The press provided no further reports of the investigation, and later bookmaking investigations in the 1950s also went nowhere.

From 1948 until I defeated him in 1970, King County's prosecutor was Carroll, whose tenure in office neatly maps onto the era of the Tolerance Policy, and whose departure marked its end. The episode of the small-time bookie illustrates Carroll's approach toward the control of vice. Carroll might show concern or make a stab at an investigation, but in the end, nothing ever happened. During his twenty-two years as prosecuting attorney, Carroll decided who would be charged with a crime and, more importantly, who wouldn't. Under his aegis, the purveyors of vice were rarely harassed, and corrupt police were left undisturbed. Graft flourished even as Carroll himself grew ever more powerful politically.

In Seattle, Carroll's roots went far back. His father opened Carroll's Fine Jewelry in 1895, which survived 113 years. (Its large sidewalk clock currently graces the front steps of Seattle's Museum of History and Industry.) Carroll's most enduring claim to fame occurred before he entered politics—he was one hell of a football player. Carroll played for the UW Huskies in the 1920s and was their star halfback, running back, and linebacker, nationally ranked. He would have contended for a Heisman Trophy if it had existed. When Carroll described football, he might also have been describing his political philosophy: "I loved it. You'd stand behind the line of scrimmage, and it was either him or you." All his life, Carroll carried himself like a former football star—smiling, confident, broad-shouldered. His short hair would turn silver, his countenance more ruddy, but he never lost the ability to dominate those near him.

Carroll became chair of the Young Republicans in 1936, and in 1938, at the age of thirty-two, he ran for King County prosecutor, losing in the primary. After the war, during which he served in the Army JAG Corps, Carroll continued to be interested in politics. In 1946, Ross Cunningham mentioned Carroll as a possible candidate for Congress. In 1948, Charles O. Carroll went to the trouble of paying for ads stating he was not related to "Charles M. Carroll," who was then in a successful run for city council.

Carroll ended up King County prosecuting attorney by appointment. In November 1948, Prosecutor Lloyd Shorett was elected a superior court judge, and the county commissioners made Carroll his successor by a 2–1 vote along party lines. The dissenting Democrat and the municipal league asked the commissioners to heed contrary recommendations of the Seattle Bar Association. With a sweeping logic, Commissioner Bill Sears responded that any lawyer who was a member of the Seattle Bar Association had the talent to serve as prosecutor.

Carroll's first moves in office confirmed his partisan leanings. He immediately announced he would replace existing personnel in the office with "outstanding Republicans screened through the Republican county central committee."

## Carroll and the Tolerance Policy

Carroll had no part in creating the Tolerance Policy and never publicly endorsed it. To the contrary, he rejected the concept of tolerating vice and, at least initially, made a show of cracking down on gambling. Shortly after his appointment, he stated he would investigate gambling establishments himself but then accepted Chief Eastman's promise to eliminate cash-paying punchboards. In January 1949, on reports that six gambling establishments had opened up following his appointment, Carroll threatened to take his deputies and raid the joints personally, darkly suggesting San Francisco Chinese were behind the gambling shops. Carroll eventually ordered the sheriff, Harlan Callahan, to raid a Chinese gambling joint. Six were arrested, while two others fled out a back door. The press revealed no further follow-up. Carroll's public denouncements of gambling soon died away.

Carroll swiftly became part of the team setting the borders of tolerance. In September 1949, Carroll and Chief Eastman agreed to limit football gambling, including placing caps on amounts and prohibiting bets on high school games. In December 1949, Carroll worked with the county commissioners to craft a response to a Washington Supreme Court opinion finding pinball machines were gambling devices.

Carroll recommended changing the licensing ordinance to forbid any type of payout, by the machine or otherwise. The commission took his advice but was careful to cushion the blow to the pinball industry. Fees charged to pinball license owners in Seattle were reduced to compensate for the anticipated loss of income, from $12.50 per machine to $2.50 per machine.

In a few months, some machines that automatically made payouts crept back into use, and in May 1950, a Seattle judge held that a player who racked up ninety-six free games on one machine could get ninety-six nickels to play on a different machine. Mayor Devin expressed concern that players might pocket those nickels instead of playing the free games but said the city would adopt a policy of watchful waiting to see if pinball players abused the situation. Carroll said nothing at all. As it played out, the watchers mostly just waited. Right through the sixties, pinball players winning free games had no problem getting cash equivalents.

As he settled into office, Carroll's passivity toward vice and corruption was criticized. In 1958, the young Brock Adams challenged Carroll for election, claiming the prosecutor did not act vigorously enough to charge national Teamster leader Dave Beck, who lived in Seattle, for embezzling Teamster funds. Adams promised to investigate Seattle's recent scandals and prevent a drift to corruption. But Carroll survived Adams's challenge, though by the smallest margin of his five election victories.

In 1961, a private attorney, Henry Opendack, confronted Carroll's passivity more directly. Opendack represented a woman arrested for distributing football gambling cards in the Richelieu Café, a cocktail lounge on Union Street. Although football betting cards were illegal, the city stamped and licensed baseball betting cards. Police chief Frank Ramon explained the distinction to the press: the Seattle police could control the distribution of baseball and other sports cards, but football cards came from elsewhere, possibly Chicago.

In his client's defense, Opendack claimed the city was arbitrarily distinguishing between types of gambling. And he was a determined attorney. He initiated a separate lawsuit, attempting to force Carroll to seize all punchboards, spindle devices, and sports cards, not just the football cards. To back up his complaint, Opendack provided evidence of seven taverns with open gambling.

Opendack's motivations are not obvious; his initial client, Ms. Kiersey, was not part of this lawsuit. Instead, Opendack's complaint was briefly joined by a contractor, Norkel Tilson, who said he was motivated by his Christian beliefs. For his trouble, Tilson received bomb threats.

But Opendack persisted until June 1962, repeatedly appearing in court to demand a decision regarding the legality of the tolerated gambling in Seattle, while Deputy Prosecutor Joel Rindal appeared to fend Opendack off. After June, Opendack's lawsuit disappeared from the papers.

As Opendack pressed his claims, Carroll made a public show of opposing gambling. But it was just show. In December 1961, in response to a preliminary ruling in the Opendack suit, Carroll and the sheriff, Tim McCullough, announced all punchboards would be withdrawn from the county by January 1. But McCullough quickly changed his mind after a meeting with some concerned tavern owners and a later private meeting with Carroll. The sheriff postponed banning punchboards until after Seattle decided what to do inside the city. Nothing further happened.

Carroll became so identified with the Tolerance Policy not by publicly supporting it but by not disturbing it. At all times, he claimed himself ready to prosecute any vice charge brought to him by the police or the sheriff, but he expressed little interest in pushing for such charges to be brought. The Tolerance Policy's supporters saw him as their ally, particularly the *Seattle Times'* Ross Cunningham. A conservative himself, Cunningham was predisposed to support a fellow conservative Republican. But he had a special love for Carroll.

Based on his own sources, Cunningham believed Carroll was key to blocking national crime figures from operating in Seattle. In 1962, when Carroll was running for reelection, the municipal league voted to give him a lesser rating than his opponent — "above average" instead of "superior." Cunningham rushed to the league office and persuaded the board to hold a special evening meeting to change the vote, passionately arguing that the league failed to appropriately value Carroll's role in keeping Seattle off limits to the national Mafia. Sometimes Cunningham would hint broadly that Carroll's tactics included throwing gangsters into Lake Washington.

In the 1962 election, Carroll's opponent was lawyer Dan Brink who ran ads excoriating Carroll for allowing the Tolerance Policy to continue for so many years. They were to no avail. Carroll won overwhelmingly, as he had before and would again.

## The Golden Years of Tolerance

Devin and Eastman created the Tolerance Policy to guide the police in their enforcement of existing vice laws, but over time it came to mean much more. At City Hall, the Tolerance Policy supported city ordinances licensing card rooms, pinball machines, and assorted "trade stimulants"—for example, punchboards and baseball cards. The Tolerance Policy reassured the purchasers of licenses that they wouldn't be arrested. The licensing ordinances did not explicitly condone betting and theoretically were trumped by state laws against gambling, but everyone understood that the police would be guided by city regulations, not state law.

The city council supported licensing ordinances in part because they allowed the city to keep local control over vice. But even more significant were financial dividends, for the city and for councilmembers. License fees and associated taxes for pinball machines and card rooms, as well as lesser "amusement devices" such as baseball cards, generated significant city revenue—around $500,000 per year during the sixties. Ending the Tolerance Policy meant ending these fees, and through the fifties and sixties, city councilmembers were tight-fisted businessmen who preferred imposing license fees to raising taxes.

In addition, by regulating gambling, the city council ensured campaign contributions from gambling operators interested in the regulations. Seattle City Council elections were low-dollar affairs, and a few thousand could be highly useful, particularly if acquired at the last minute with a couple of phone calls, when other sources were tapped out.

Gambling interests also provided councilmembers with perks. Charles M. "Streetcar Charlie" Carroll spoke openly to the press about the benefits of being on the city council, including receiving "free-ers," such as dinners or junkets. A high-ranking police officer named Anton "Tony" Gustin later claimed in an interview that the police were once forced to pressure a business into providing one needy city councilmember with matching luggage. Of course, some gambling money might simply have gone straight into councilmember pockets. There are numerous rumors on this point from the era, though they are frustratingly hard to pin down.

In *Seattle Vice*, Rick Anderson notes one intriguing episode. US Attorney Brock Adams, in the course of cracking down on gambling in 1962, wiretapped conversations between Bill Colacurcio (brother to the more notorious Frank Colacurcio) and others involved in pinball operations. Bill refused to answer questions about the recording before the grand jury and ended up in jail for contempt, for at least a few hours, before breaking down and testifying. Whatever Bill said is still sealed in grand jury records somewhere. But according to Anderson, who spoke to someone in the 1970s who was associated with the Colacurcios, the recording detailed payoffs being made both to the police and to select city councilmembers.

## An Invitation to Corruption

The city council's licensing ordinances required police cooperation. No one would buy licenses if they did not protect against arrest. And the police had their own reasons to support the Tolerance Policy.

Like the city council, the police liked the control provided by licensing ordinances. A system that all but openly made the police judges of what laws would be enforced suited them fine. Senior officers commanded great power over businesses operating in Pioneer Square and elsewhere. The police vice squad recommended to the city council which card rooms or pinball-license holders should retain or lose their licenses, and city councilmembers usually took the advice. Licenses kept outsiders out and gave insiders power.

The Tolerance Policy also encouraged the police to practice their own version of self-interested licensing by demanding payoffs. Whatever a mayor might say in public, the actual working of the Tolerance Policy carried its own message—lawbreaking would be tolerated for the money. So why shouldn't the police do the same?

Fundamentally, the Tolerance Policy was an official endorsement of municipal corruption. In the pursuit of license fees, the city told the police to arrest only some criminals, regardless of state law. For years, police chiefs like Kimsey or Lawrence had welcomed this kind of direction. In the words of veteran political observer Ross Cunningham, the chiefs told mayors and city councils, "tell us what kind of town you want, and we'll adjust accordingly." Even earlier, there had been Chief Wappenstein's overenthusiastic carrying out of Mayor Gill's plans for an open city—Wappenstein had understood this to mean "anything goes." Senior officers believed law enforcement depended less on what the laws said and more on the desires of particular mayors or councils, as interpreted by the police.

In theory, the Tolerance Policy removed temptation from individual officers by setting clear limits on licensed gambling. In practice, police discretion still determined whether an establishment survived or not. Early on, Devin and Eastman decided a one-dollar limit on card games sufficed. But at this level, card rooms found it difficult to make a profit. To the extent any card games continued to heed one-dollar limits, it was principally to identify gamblers who could be lured into playing higher-dollar games. As for taverns, the intricate regulations propounded by the Washington State Liquor Control Board limiting the size of rooms, the proportion of liquor to food, and the hours when liquor could be served could not all be obeyed if the owner still wished to make any money. The police did not have the manpower or interest to fully enforce the vice laws, but the laws remained available as needed to coerce payoffs.

Police officers made regular calls on taverns, card rooms, dance halls, and public baths, demanding monthly contributions from licensed establishments. Unlike the Mob, Seattle's police force did not enforce its demands by burning down buildings or breaking legs but used quieter methods. Businesses that refused to pay would be harassed by the police, who would enforce code violations or relentlessly request identification from customers, until the business lost enough money to change its mind.

Not that all these businesses consistently opposed payoffs. One officer recalls that bars who paid him off assumed that gave them a right to complain about competitors who didn't and to get the police to shut them down. For a period, large numbers of bar owners seemed to accept payoffs as one more level of licensing—the police tax. But over time, police demands for payoffs would escalate, driving more and more business owners to rebellion.

## Sex and Drugs

The payoff system extorting Seattle's bars and card rooms was only the most visible part of the graft. The Tolerance Policy distinguished between major and minor vice, and theoretically only licensed gambling was on the tolerated side. But untolerated vice still managed to survive.

Brothels had not been officially tolerated since Mayor Gill, and in the wake of federal intervention during World War II, even unofficial tolerance faded away. The most notorious public houses moved to smaller cities, such as Aberdeen. One of the last to leave was the LaSalle Hotel, above the Pike Place Market, which survived to the early fifties. The man who bought it in 1951, George Ikeda, thought he was actually buying a hotel. He later sued for breach of contract when it became clear there were no actual overnight guests to speak of but instead thirty to forty men who arrived each day looking for prostitutes. By the 1960s, houses of prostitution tended to be just that: discreet houses found up the hill from downtown Seattle. Their existence was reasonably well known, but they rarely suffered police interference. Anecdotal accounts indicate the managers paid for their protection.

And vice always seeks new markets. By the sixties, Seattle had developed a healthy array of satellite versions of sex for money—striptease joints and peepshows. Like Pioneer Square's gay bars, bathhouses, and dance halls, these all operated in their own legal gray area, and like every other business in that gray zone, they were subject to police demands for money.

## How Much Money?

What made the system work were the enormous profits of Seattle's vice industry, easily sufficient to support license fees, taxes, campaign contributions, and police payoffs. It's difficult to get numbers for some parts of the system—for example, drugs and prostitution. Big-money card games were also sufficiently illegal that any numbers associated with them are speculative. But more minor gambling was licensed and taxed, allowing some tracking.

Pinball machines, for example, were extremely lucrative, and profits generated by pinball reached as high as $25 million per year in 1964, worth approximately $188.5 million today. Bingo games, run by both church groups and more shady "nonprofits" cleared up to $1.5 million per year in Seattle and King County in the late sixties. Card rooms cleared millions more. And these are only the official numbers. It was an open secret that revenues reported for purposes of taxes and license fees were a fraction of the fees legally due.

From time to time, skimming became obvious. In the 1950s, an enterprising fellow created his own version of the city's official stamp used to certify pulltabs and started stamping the pulltabs of taverns and bars for a fee. He kept it up until eventually somebody noticed license revenues had taken a sudden dip. He told investigators he shared some of the money with city staff. But mostly, skimming was shrugged off. When I discussed these days with Dan Evans, Washington's governor during the sixties, he noted the city was probably only receiving one-tenth of the money it was owed.

Estimates of gross gambling profits for the state are thus uncertain, but some claimed they ranged from $50 to $100 million per year in the sixties. By comparison, Boeing's net earnings for 1965 were $78 million. Washington stood out in the United States for its levels of gambling, at least on paper. The federal government required gambling operators to buy federal gambling stamps and pay gambling revenues. In other parts of the country, doing so exposed gamblers to arrest for violation of local laws. In Seattle, that wasn't a problem, and in 1961 approximately one-third of all wagering stamps purchased in the country were bought in Washington.

## Defending the City

Defenders of the Tolerance Policy claimed it kept Seattle free of "real" mobsters. Real mobsters made their most direct challenge from 1958 to 1960. During these years there were five bombings of pinball machines or vendors, at least officially, though there's reason to think some bombings may have been unrecorded. Someone used sticks of dynamite to blow up pinball machines or cars and buildings associated with pinball operators. Nobody got hurt.

At the time the bombings were a great mystery, causing public head scratching by the police. Many years later, the responsibility is pretty clear. In Seattle, the pinball business was essentially a cartel of forty to fifty people who owned licenses allowing rental of pinball machines. Frank Colacurcio and his brother Bill wanted to break into this business and take it over by pressuring bar owners to take Colacurcio machines, instead of using those from the opposing group of established operators. Pressure took the form of explosions.

But the Tolerance Policy was up to the challenge. The imagined enemy had been Chicago gangsters, not the homegrown sort, but the Colacurcios still found themselves stymied. The Seattle City Council held hearings and took away the pinball and jukebox licenses from the Colacurcios. Frank reacted by moving into strip joints instead, while Bill eventually left town.

The city council, meanwhile, continued to protect the monopoly on pinball licenses that kept profits high. Ostensibly concerned that allowing individual bar owners to own pinball machines would cause destructive competition with those currently owning the machines, the council prevented those who owned licenses from owning pinball locations and vice versa. The council then limited the number of licenses available at any one time. Jukebox licensing proceeded along similar lines, and later the council attempted to regulate placement and ownership of coin-operated pool tables. A limited number of licenses for entertainment devices kept power in the hands of the city council to oversee the holders of licenses, discouraging them from setting off pipe bombs. But it also encouraged license holders to protect their monopolies through generous campaign contributions.

## Ignoring the Complainers

A bigger threat to the Tolerance Policy than dynamite was citizen complaints by those who lost money gambling or were forced to make payoffs. Men sometimes managed to lose hundreds of dollars in Seattle's card rooms, even with one-dollar limits. Some complained to the police, or at least their angry wives did, resulting in temporary suspensions of card room licenses, though little else.

Tavern owners and card room licensees who resented making payoffs were more persistent complainers. Some attempted to take their complaints to a police captain or chief, or the prosecutor.

These complaints normally went nowhere and had no effect. Few had the stamina to take it further.

One such man who did was Charles McNeal, the hapless purchaser of the tavern Battersby & Smith in 1957. He was immediately harassed into paying off the police for the privilege of operating a card room. After complying for some time, he ceased paying and was driven out of the business by 1961. Before going, he posted a large sign in his window stating:

THIS RESTAURANT HAS BEEN FORCED TO CLOSE BECAUSE I REFUSED TO JOIN THE GAMBLING SYNDICATE AND I REFUSED TO BE FORCED INTO FURTHER PAYMENTS OF EXTORTION MONIES TO THE PROTECTION RACKET WHOSE ENFORCERS ARE CERTAIN MEMBERS OF THE POLICE FORCE.

I HAVE ISSUED A PUBLIC CHALLENGE TO THOSE WHOM I HAVE ACCUSED OF THESE ATROCITIES—TO TAKE A TEST OF TRUTH—A TEST THEY DARE NOT TAKE—A LIE DETECTOR TEST. I HAVE AGREED TO TAKE SUCH A TEST, THE GREAT WHITE CHIEF AND THE LORD HIGH MAYOR HAVE NOT ACCEPTED, THEY DARE NOT ACCEPT.

McNeal also held a news conference and later testified in front of a committee of the state legislature. No action resulted.

When some external event did force an investigation, the results evaporated in a fog of ineffectuality. In 1955, after reports that the police force was racially biased, Mayor Pomeroy formed a citizens' committee to investigate: the Advisory Committee on Police Practices, headed by the Very Reverend John Leffler, dean of Saint Mark's Episcopal Cathedral. The committee soon became intrigued by a report from the Federal Bureau of Narcotics stating that narcotics were not a significant problem in Seattle except among blacks but that investigation of the problem was hampered because bars in the predominantly African American Central District paid off the police.

Leffler's committee asked the police to come to meetings and answer questions. The police refused with the exception of a Captain Cook, who denied everything. The committee issued a report noting their frustration and suggesting the police might have problems in areas like brutality, racial discrimination, and corruption. It then disbanded.

## Scenes from the Seattle Night circa the 1960s

The Tolerance Policy was a theory. In practice, what was life actually like in Seattle's downtown? Some middle-class observers dipped their toes in the murky waters and returned to provide accounts.

In 1960, following the wave of pinball bombings, an intrepid reporter at the *Seattle Times* took twenty-five dollars of his paper's money and attempted to see how long he could last playing pinball. He moved from one pinball machine to another among the hundreds found in the bars and cigar stores of downtown Seattle and went broke in a little less than two weeks, though the bar owners always readily paid off his free games in cash. He observed that pinball looked like a way to win money but that doing so was nearly impossible. He also noted how addictive playing the machines had become.

*Seattle* magazine was a short-lived local experiment in investigative journalism, progressive politics, and protohipster attitude founded by Stimson Bullitt, the son of broadcasting pioneer Dorothy Bullitt, in 1964. In 1967, its editors were intrigued by statements made by officials at Fort Lewis that Seattle had more locations off limits to soldiers than any other Pacific Coast city, including eleven taverns, one café, five hotels, and two steam baths. *Seattle* sent out a journalist to visit these dens of iniquity and report back. The story is entertaining—the reporter beat a hasty retreat from one steam room when the other young men there began taking off their towels and giving him searching looks. Mostly, though, the reporter describes one dingy tavern and card room after another, where police interest or interference was nonexistent.

But the most detailed description of Seattle's underworld comes via a sociologist, William Chambliss of the University of Washington. In the early sixties, as a graduate student, he investigated Seattle's downtown as a test case for sociological theories regarding municipal government. He spent long hours observing Seattle's bars, card rooms, and peepshows with the clinical detachment of an anthropologist documenting an Amazon tribe. He dropped nickels into pinball machines and cashed in the free games. He hung around with others at peepshows and learned the trick of how to view the most explicit images at the lowest price. He played cards in card rooms and watched the staff entice heavy bettors into playing elsewhere for higher stakes. He watched police officers walk out of bars with paper bags of money and reported rumors of murders committed to silence those who might expose the graft. He interviewed aggrieved card room licensee Charles McNeal at length about his long, grim failed struggle to get anybody to take his complaints seriously.

After years of field research and interviews with anonymous bartenders, prostitutes, police officers, and businessmen, Chambliss reached a conclusion—Seattle was systematically corrupt. He claimed the troubles went past payoffs and included police rings peddling stolen merchandise, respectable businessmen financing drug transactions, and respectable companies, like the *Seattle Times*, bribing the county assessor for favorable tax assessments. He described money from gambling put in suitcases and flown down to San Francisco on a regular basis for transfer to national crime figures. Above it all, he described a loosely organized group of local politicians and law enforcement officials controlling and profiting from the system, devoting a special section of his report to King County's prosecuting attorney. In Chambliss's account, the bars, card rooms, and bingo parlors of Seattle were all just the lowest and most visible part of one large con game, in which crooks fleeced the suckers and the police ignored it all for a price—when they weren't harassing businessmen for more money.

The book Chambliss wrote about his investigation, *On the Take: From Petty Crooks to Presidents*, starts with Seattle but by the halfway point segues into lurid descriptions of national and international corruption, indicating the author's conspiratorial imagination. And even regarding Seattle, Chambliss's reporting is sloppy. His account often fails to name specific individuals or dates, appears to take on faith every story told to him, and is otherwise difficult to verify. At a couple of points, Chambliss just gets his facts wrong—for example, describing the *Seattle Times* as a Hearst-owned paper. But there is no doubt Chambliss walked the streets of Seattle in the early sixties, sat in the bars and card rooms, talked to the gamblers and their friends, observed the behavior of police, and faithfully recorded the stories he was told. Even if only some of the stories were true, they describe a dark and tainted city. They also describe a city where the perception of corruption was omnipresent.

## The World's Fair

In the summer of 1962, Seattle hosted its World's Fair, the Century 21 Exposition, rightly considered a transformative event. It marked a break in Seattle's sense of itself—the point when it consciously stepped out into the modern world. Yet the fair also reflected Seattle's divided culture: the fairgrounds contained both exhibitions of high-minded art and science and, off in the northeast corner, an "adult entertainment section," complete with the seminude Girls of the Galaxy. And whatever its long-term significance for transforming the city's culture, the fair's immediate impact on the Tolerance Policy was minimal.

The fair did require the city to do more fine-tuning of the borders of allowable vice. Prosecutor Carroll and Police Chief Frank Ramon decided a cruise liner/casino could not dock in Seattle over the course of the fair—thus competing with downtown card rooms—because "possession of gambling equipment was illegal." There was also much back and forth among officials as to which games of skill would be allowed in the sideshows or the limits of allowable undress by the Girls of the Galaxy. But none of this altered policies in the rest of the city.

It was only after the fair ended that Mayor Clinton decided to suspend the Tolerance Policy. And it was not the fair that pushed him to this step but a certain ambitious US attorney.

## Clinton Tries His Best

Clinton was elected on a platform of reform, and he gave it a shot. Soon after his election in 1956, he used his investigative fund to inquire into reports of police corruption, which caused at least some police officers to temporarily suspend payoffs. But Clinton never went public with his findings, and payoffs quickly resumed. Like Eastman, Clinton shied from confronting the department directly. In 1960, when Chief Lawrence chose to retire, the resulting exam for police chief turned up two top candidates, one from outside Seattle and the other Assistant Chief Frank Ramon. Without much resistance, Clinton bowed to departmental pressure and made Ramon chief.

Clinton's reelection in 1960 was one of the few mayoral contests up to that point where vice was not a leading campaign issue—or at least it wasn't until a week before the election, when somebody bombed the car of Clinton's opponent Gordon Newell. Given the other fire bombings of the previous two years, suspicion immediately focused on pinball operators. Newell claimed he was bombed because in recent weeks he had been calling for an end to the pinball monopoly in Seattle. But no one could explain why anyone would bother to bomb a losing candidate in a hopeless campaign. The less charitable gossiped that Newell had bombed his own car for the publicity.

But though he shied from confronting the police, by the beginning of his second term, Clinton was willing to take on the Tolerance Policy. In the summer of 1960, Clinton pointed to the various pinball bombings over the past two years as evidence that the policy was not working to control crime. He announced an ultimatum: if the police did not solve the bombings by August, he would end the Tolerance Policy by ending city licensing of minor gambling. The deadline came and went without the police cracking the case, and Clinton asked the city council to end licensing. City councilmembers, aghast at the possible revenue loss, rejected the idea.

Clinton waited another year before trying again. On the eve of the coming World's Fair, in January 1962, he proposed that the city council end licensing of pinball machines, punchboards, and card rooms. His argument was that although the Tolerance Policy might have once been needed when the police were inadequate to control gambling, the police force was now capable of doing so. City councilmembers, still aghast, pigeonholed the proposal.

The matter might have rested with the pigeons, but that May young US Attorney Brock Adams led FBI raids of Seattle gambling locations, arresting several proprietors for possession of gambling equipment (for example, roulette wheels or dice) transported across state lines. The headlines spurred Clinton to renew his call to end the Tolerance Policy. The council remained aghast and did nothing.

Clinton lost patience. On June 22, he took an unprecedented end run around the council. He announced that as of January 1, the police would be directed to end illegal gambling where it was found, *whether or not* the proprietors held licenses.

The immediate council reaction was defiant—a majority was willing to renew all the licenses anyway, hoping to still collect the revenue. By December, cooler heads sought compromise. The new reform-minded members of the council, Wing Luke and Lud Kramer, proposed that the city only license punchboard and pinball machines that were stripped of any cash rewards—they would be "for amusement purposes only." Mayor Clinton welcomed the notion but made it clear that it would not alter his edict—beginning in 1963 possession of a license of any sort would not protect gambling.

In the fall of 1962, the city sent two thousand certified letters to the proprietors of the city's licensed bars, card rooms, and smoke shops warning that come January 1, gambling laws would be fully enforced. And, as promised, when the new year arrived, there were some arrests and prosecutions, dutifully chronicled by the press. The market for city licenses took a drastic downturn, drying up city revenue.

But Clinton's determination to end city licensing of minor gambling met an immediate backlash, demonstrating just how entrenched gambling interests had become in Washington's politics and incidentally leading to one of the state's most spectacular political crimes.

## The Great Referendum Robbery

In the spring of 1963, legislators in Olympia moved quickly to reverse Clinton's suspension of the Tolerance Policy. They passed a bill making some gambling legal in Washington by local option. But a minister in Tacoma then filed a referendum to overturn the law, quickly gathering twice the needed signatures to put the issue on the ballot. The petitions were stored in the vault of the office of the Washington secretary of state, Vic Meyers, to await verification.

In the twenties, the colorful Meyers had been a great band leader. In the thirties and forties, he was an entertaining and minimally competent lieutenant governor. But his last political job, serving as secretary of state, proved more difficult, and his talents did not extend to vault security. Sometime on a Friday evening in June 1963, two men broke into his office, cracked the vault, and hauled eighty thousand petition signatures off into the night. A night cleaner observed the two men take the signatures but did not regard it worth reporting, so the robbery was not discovered until the following Monday. There was widespread suspicion that this was an inside job, though reporters noted the vault was hardly impervious—its combination had not been changed for twenty years.

The thieves were never caught and have not been identified since, but their work was for naught. The hapless Meyers agreed with Governor Rosellini to hold the vote even though the signatures had not been verified. The filing of the referendum suspended the implementation of the new gambling tolerance law until after a vote at the next general election in November 1964, but at least as regards Seattle, the issue soon became moot. Mayor Clinton's strict enforcement of antigambling laws was his own mayoral initiative, and in the spring of 1964, Seattle got a new mayor.

## Tolerance Returns

Dorm Braman, previously an influential city councilmember, became mayor on a platform that included restoring the Tolerance Policy and an open town. (Though a more important issue was whether the city should end racial discrimination in housing. Braman opposed the proposed open-housing measure on the ballot, which went down to defeat.)

In those days, mayoral elections took place in spring, and on March 10, 1964, Braman reversed Clinton's suspension of fourteen months before. With city council concurrence, he immediately directed police to return to ignoring low-level gambling sanctioned by possession of a city license. The resurrected Tolerance Policy would remain in effect until 1969.

It's not clear if Clinton's brief suspension of the Tolerance Policy actually changed much. The police raided a few card rooms and cigar stores, but there's little evidence this affected overall rates of gambling and there's no evidence police payoffs stopped in 1963. The same police force that took payoffs to leave licensed card rooms alone continued taking payoffs to leave unlicensed card rooms alone. The principle effect of Clinton's move was to eliminate licensing revenue.

## Referendum 34

More than a year after the Great Referendum Robbery, Referendum 34 finally came to a vote, on the November 1964 ballot. It would provide municipalities statewide with the option of legalizing small-scale gambling, like pinball machines and card rooms—in a word, formalizing Seattle's Tolerance Policy. For those pushing the local option, the fundamental logic was consistency—it was not good policy to criminalize gambling that was widely practiced and widely tolerated. The referendum's principal financial backers, primarily gambling organizations, hoped the local option would allow them more scope for operations in the state. But their advertising pitch was that enacting gambling tolerance laws statewide would keep "professional gamblers" out of the state.

On the other side, a coalition of church groups and the *Seattle Times* feared the new law would leave the state wide open. Ross Cunningham issued a dark warning that gambling forces would pay to incorporate towns near major cities, purely for the purposes of turning them into gambling sanctuaries. Cunningham admitted rejecting the new law in the referendum vote would leave matters just as they were, including Seattle's toleration of minor gambling. But he claimed the local gamblers were firmly under local control.

In the end, morality and hypocrisy defeated gambling money and consistency. Referendum 34 lost badly, and Washington's laws remained what they had been. Voters were opposed to official statewide tolerance policies, but that did not require a significant change in Seattle's homegrown version. After meeting with local law enforcement, Braman told the press, "We will continue, as we have in the past, to enforce all laws to the degree consistent with available manpower."

Under Mayor Braman, the city returned to its usual ways. Seattle would tolerate some open vice but not too much. The city would make money by licensing gambling but only pinball machines, card rooms, and varieties of punchboards and spindles glossed over as "trade stimulant devices." If there was crime, graft, and corruption going on, at least those at fault would be local, not the Mafia figures that haunted imaginations.

# CHAPTER 3

# REFORM COMES TO TOWN

★ ★ ★ ★ ★ ★ ★ ★ ★ ★ ★ ★

I've been a political junkie since the fourth grade, when I violated Washington gambling laws by losing a dime on the Truman-Dewey race. Four years later, I was very excited about General Dwight Eisenhower, and as luck would have it, there was a Republican precinct caucus across the lawn in Uncle Mike and Aunt Ginna's basement during the big 1952 GOP primary fight. My indulgent relatives let their activist nephew not only attend but participate. This fourteen-year-old ended up debating a conservative neighbor, retired vice admiral Alan Smith, who was firmly for Senator Robert Taft.

We lived in the Broadview neighborhood, recently annexed to Seattle when the city limits moved from 85th Street to 145th Street. Downtown was very far away, and we were actually in the Shoreline School District. I did what passed for student politics at the brand-new Jane Addams Junior High School way east in Lake City, and after that I bussed or—after getting my license—drove my 1947 Plymouth seven miles in to Lincoln High School to complete my public-school education.

My group at Lincoln was the "smart kids," who ran things from debate to journalism. I ended up editor of the *Lincoln Totem* and remember selling an ad to Dick Spady just before he opened his first drive-in several blocks east of school, now the eponymous and locally famous Dick's Drive-In chain. Some of us were athletes, and we were proud to be the 1955 Washington State high school basketball champs. My contribution to that was helping star forward Herb Brightenborn navigate Mr. Frizzel's physics class. My first venture in elective politics was a failure—I lost the position of student council representative-at-large to Marilyn Berg, a longstanding member of the Lincoln leadership cadre.

My chief claim to fame before college was winning the 1956 Teenage Safe-Driving Roadeo, beating out forty-seven state winners in a test of driving skills. I entered it hoping to win a car, but they changed the rules that year and my prize was a $1,500 scholarship.

I went to Harvard College in 1956 and joined the Harvard Young Republican Club just in time for a bitter intratribal fight among various factions for leadership. I was elected president of the HYRC as a junior and in the process met fellow Seattleite Tom Alberg and his roommate, future Seattle City Councilmember Bruce Chapman. Both would help me later on.

In June 1960, I reported aboard USS *Abbot* (DD-629), a destroyer, to fulfill my three-year NROTC active-duty obligation. This meant following the presidential campaign from afar, including listening to the Nixon-Kennedy debates on reel-to-reel tapes sent from home. I was back in Cambridge for law school in time to join in the founding of the Ripon Society, a self-described think tank for young Republicans modeled on the conservative Bow Group in England. We battled the forces of Barry Goldwater over civil and voting rights in the South and went down in dismal defeat at the Republican National Convention in San Francisco in 1964.

I returned to Seattle in 1966 and started my legal career with Lane, Powell, Moss & Miller that summer. But like in college and law school, politics was the siren song. And I arrived at a good time, because some of Seattle's political reformers were just beginning the first of a series of movements that would permanently change

Seattle's political Establishment. And, strangely enough, the first issue we tackled was Sunday drinking.

## Fighting for a Sunday Cocktail

Imagine it's Saturday night in Seattle and you are enjoying a late dinner at Victor Rosellini's fabled 410, one of Seattle's few real restaurants. But then the clock strikes twelve. Before 1966, the waiter would appear and remove your half-empty wine bottle and glasses, citing a state law forbidding the purchase, sale, or consumption of alcohol on Sunday.

This particular rule stemmed from the 1909 Sabbath Breaking Law. The Liquor Control Board, established to regulate alcohol after 1933, determined that the sale of liquor on a Sunday was forbidden. In the midsixties, there were only three fancy restaurants in Seattle: Rosellini's 410 in the White-Henry-Stuart Building, Canlis on its perch overlooking Lake Union, where it is today; and the Marine Room in the Olympic Hotel. Today's bustling restaurant scene might have never happened if the no booze on Sunday rule had remained.

Although I helped the effort out, the heroes of the battle for Sunday drinking were an unlikely pair of young political activists who met while clerking for justices of the Washington Supreme Court.

Lem Howell would one day become one of Seattle's premier civil rights attorneys, bringing numerous lawsuits challenging discrimination and police misconduct. But he began a little more sedately. In 1964, as a twenty-eight-year-old NYU law grad, Howell received a Ford Foundation grant to work for the reelection of Governor Rosellini against his challenger, young Dan Evans. After Rosellini lost, Howell intended to move back to New York, but fate intervened when Burt Johnson in the governor's office introduced

Howell to the justices of the state supreme court. Justice Frank Weaver hired him as a law clerk, and Howell never looked back.

While on the court, Howell socialized with fellow law clerk Camden Hall. Hall's roots were more local. He grew up in Seattle, went to Ballard High, and then moved across town to the University of Washington to become ASUW (Associated Students of the University of Washington) president in 1962. During law school at UW, Hall worked for Nelson Rockefeller's 1964 presidential campaign, and you'll still find a big grinning photo of Rocky, signed to Hall, on the wall of his law office in downtown Seattle today. In 1965, Hall started working for Justice Orris Hamilton. Though nominally of different parties, Howell and Hall bonded over politics; at the time, reformers in both the Democratic and Republican parties shared some common interests in changing politics.

In the course of the 1964 campaign, Howell met many like-minded young politicos and ended up leading the state Young Democrats. These young activists looked for an issue to get Democrats to the polls in the 1966 off-year election. The blue laws, forbidding Sunday business, had never been particularly popular in Washington but had survived by never being seriously enforced, at least as regards general business. That changed in 1965, when the Skagit County prosecutor made a much publicized attempt to shut down the Sunday operations of a hapless car dealer. The Sunday closure law was now a ripe target, and Howell and Hall, along with their respective activist friends like me, decided to take it on.

Howell and Hall found both financial support and motivated volunteers. Funding came from restaurant owners. The Liquor Control Board took the blue laws more seriously than the state's prosecutors usually did and rigidly enforced laws against selling liquor on Sundays. Small bars might try to bribe themselves out of this problem, effectively becoming speakeasies after midnight, but larger, more respectable restaurants wanted other options.

Volunteers came from the Seventh-day Adventists, who had long chafed at the special legal status the law gave to Sunday. The Adventists took Saturday as their day of rest. Of course, the Adventists also opposed drinking regardless of the day, but they were willing to overlook this fact to end the discrimination.

Howell and Hall organized an alliance of the secular and spiritual to wage a successful petition drive. Victor Rosellini provided them an office and hosted meetings at his restaurant, which encouraged volunteer enthusiasm. For their part, the Adventists provided the bulk of the petition gatherers.

Initiative 229 got 187,463 valid signatures—more than ever previously collected in state history—ended up on the 1966 ballot, and was approved by 65.8 percent. It took another six months and some public pressure to prod the state liquor board into changing the rules and allowing Washingtonians to drink on Sundays. That happened on July 19, 1967, and Victor Rosellini could then serve drinks all night long.

Ending the blue laws helped Seattle's restaurant industry and showed that some statutes penalizing commonplace behavior had little support. It also provided a group of young politicos with valuable experience campaigning and their first success. They realized that they and their allies formed a constituency in Seattle for general political reform, not necessarily tied to one party or the other.

## CHECC Attacks Seattle's Bipartisan Problem: Its City Council

Initiative 229 was only the beginning. My next adventure began soon after, as I joined with others to reform Seattle's most obvious political problem, its city council. The council mostly consisted of colorless, nearly anonymous, and generally unimaginative older businessmen who, paradoxically, wielded nearly all municipal power. Changing Seattle politics required changing the type of councilmembers and changing the operation of the council.

The pressure for change had been building for a couple of years. Reformers Wing Luke and Lud Kramer were elected to the council in 1962 and pushed for reforms. Luke in particular was a voice criticizing Seattle's Tolerance Policy and advocating for open housing laws. But both were gone quickly: Kramer in 1964, when he replaced Vic Meyers as Washington secretary of state, and Luke, tragically, in an airplane crash in 1965. To replace these reformers, the old timers on the council appointed people like themselves, conservative white male small-business men with little interest in making significant changes. In 1965, *Seattle* magazine memorably described the group as "Our Musty, Crusty City Council." Looking back, the *P-I*'s columnist Emmett Watson was only slightly more charitable: "Taken singly, they were decent, upstanding people. Put together as a governing body of Seattle they and their predecessors, cast in a similar mold, had a bad effect on each other, like too many maple bars stuck together in a single bag."

Youngsters in Seattle's political community decided to do something about it. The "something" was CHECC (Choose an Effective City Council). One inspiration was Philip Bailey, publisher of the weekly newspaper the *Argus*. In December 1966, Bailey editorialized for "the young people of Seattle to overhaul city government." For Howell, Hall, and friends, this was welcome advice. Their group included Republicans like Hall, George Akers, Tom Alberg, and myself, as well as like-minded young Democrats like Howell; Peter LeSourd, who had worked to elect Democrat Brock Adams to Congress in 1964; Alan Munro; and Llewelyn Pritchard, a high-energy young lawyer who had recently arrived from back east. Together the group came up with CHECC, a bipartisan effort to change the city council.

I remember early CHECC meetings well. They were held in places like the fireplace room of the downtown YMCA. CHECC unleashed the energies of those of us cutting our teeth in both parties and served our ambitions to rise up Democratic and Republican ladders.

The late Dick Bushnell was our press guru. The public launch on April 24, 1967, was a great success. The room was packed with local press as, sitting shoulder to shoulder, Democrat LeSourd and Republican Hall made the pitch for reform, backed by an array of members from the Young Republicans, Metropolitan Democratic Club, and Junior Chamber of Commerce.

Looking back, it seems astonishing CHECC established such instant credibility. The *P-I*, reflecting its own progressive bias, was positive from the start, with an editorial called "Hats Off to CHECC," but even the conservative *Seattle Times* acknowledged some change might be good. And of course Phil Bailey was enthusiastic in the *Argus*. Writing later, reporter David Brewster noted one reason for CHECC's success was that CHECC said things journalists always wanted to say but had been afraid to point out under their own names.

CHECC's first endorsements were Democrat Phyllis Lamphere and Republican Tim Hill in the 1967 election. The bipartisan nature of CHECC was immediately challenged when, belatedly, a third reform candidate, Democratic state senator Sam Smith, was also proposed for a position. In a close vote, ultimately decided by LeSourd's tiebreaker, CHECC voted not to endorse anyone for the third position, preserving the one-for-one bipartisan balance. Lamphere and Hill both won, as did Smith, even without CHECC's endorsement. The net result was three new reformers on the council.

Two years later, two of CHECC's four endorsed candidates won, Liem Tuai and George Cooley. In 1971, John Miller and Bruce Chapman, a CHECC founder, were added to the council.

CHECC leader Randy Revelle was elected in 1973, nearly completing the council's transformation.

Just as the blue-law repeal, CHECC served two purposes. It forced a change in the city council that was sorely needed, and it also provided an opportunity for Seattle's reformers to work together and gain trust in their mutual abilities and goals.

CHECC itself never functioned as either a party or a political program. Because it was bipartisan, its interest was less in particular policy matters and more in freeing up the frozen gears of government. Cam Hall later said that the goal was to get people with inquiring minds in office. He wanted fresh breezes to blow and wasn't too concerned with the direction.

For me, CHECC's success was critical. It gave me a strong start in local politics, working with CHECC leaders who would later help my 1970 campaign: cochair Cam Hall; Tom Alberg, campaign coordinator and doorbelling maestro; and George Akers, who helped raise money and watch the books. CHECC also enabled friendships with like-minded Democrats like Llew Pritchard, another 1970 ally.

## Seattle City Council: An All—Powerful Bag of Maple Bars

CHECC attacked one piece of the city council problem, its membership. Running alongside this effort, other reformers attempted to limit the powers of the council itself. Strangely enough, the maple bars, as a group, basically ran the city.

The city council had both legislative and executive powers. Seattle's city charter changed frequently over the years, but from the 1930s up until 1967, one constant was that Seattle was run by an unusually strong city council only occasionally interfered with by an unusually weak mayor, an arrangement created by reformers reacting to the strong-willed, corrupt mayors of the twenties and thirties. A mayor could appoint people to office but could not always fire them without council approval. Even more significantly, Seattle's council controlled department budgets.

Council committee chairs decided how much the city would spend and dealt directly with city staff to set priorities. In 1963, finance committee chair (later mayor) Dorm Braman clarified for his committee members that funds budgeted were *not* turned over to the departments but:

> rather are administered on a daily basis by the City Council Budget Office and by the City Council Finance Committee. This simply means, in layman's language, that while the necessary amounts of money to operate the city are budgeted, they are not immediately appropriated; and no one is allowed to expend any item, even though budgeted, without again demonstrating clearly the need for expenditure.

Committee chairs prided themselves on their frugality in approving actual spending and preserving unexpended funds for some future use.

The city council's license committee exerted additional executive power. It decided whether a cabaret, card room, or pinball operator kept a license or did not. It thus held a whip hand over much of Seattle's illegal gambling, and there were several instances of it suspending the licenses of disfavored license holders, such as its suspension of the Colacurcio licenses in the late 1950s. The committee operated hand in glove with the police. After his election in 1971, Bruce Chapman succeeded Charles M. Carroll as chair of the license committee. He recalled that on his first day, a delegation from the police department's vice squad called and handed him a list of establishments to be approved in a forthcoming meeting of his committee. He told his visitors in no uncertain terms that while their advice was always welcome, in the future, the committee would be making these decisions without vice squad direction.

Up through the 1960s, although disputes over the Tolerance Policy or police corruption roiled the waters of mayoral elections, real oversight over the police department or the city's licensing department devolved to senior and long-established council chairs like David Levine, Charles M. Carroll, or Dorm Braman. All approved the Tolerance Policy; none saw police corruption as a significant concern.

CHECC was not directly involved with changing the city charter. Instead, one of Seattle's hardest-working good-government groups, the League of Women Voters, took the lead. In the 1960s, they made ending council-centric government a priority, an effort championed by Phyllis Lamphere. A state bill to give Seattle's mayor budget powers finally passed the legislature in 1967, in time for Lamphere's own election to city council, endorsed by CHECC. One of the senators helping Lamphere was young Wes Uhlman, who set his sights on the newly powerful mayoral office and was elected in 1969. Lamphere later wrote that she had no regrets about limiting council power at the same time that she joined the council; depriving councilmembers power over day-to-day spending decisions provided them with more time and energy to look at larger policy questions regarding Seattle's government.

## Action for Washington—Reform Goes Republican

After CHECC, I found it hard to return to quietly drafting debentures at Lane, Powell, Moss & Miller in the Washington Building. The temptation to return to politics came in late 1967 with a call from a young WSU alum named Sam Sumner Reed. Reed had read a Ripon Society book I helped write on the 1964 election and saw I was from Seattle. Unlike CHECC, the new political outing we discussed would be partisan.

Reed had served in the Evans administration and under Secretary of State Lud Kramer, and would later become one of Kramer's distinguished successors. Like others in the Evans camp, Reed hoped to extend the success of the governor's moderate Republican administration. Together we started brainstorming about organizing young people behind Republican candidates statewide in 1968.

We formed a political group in the fall of 1967 but didn't come up with the name Action for Washington (AFW) until the following spring. We were determined to keep AFW autonomous from the Republican Party and statewide GOP campaigns. But we saw Dan Evans and Slade Gorton as models of what progressive reform looked like, and made their election our mission.

We hit on the idea of hiring college students who had the political bug and also needed to make some summer money. Seattle businessmen Shef Phelps and John Hauberg agreed to fund the plan, and with their financial help, we paid ten interns $1,000 each for the summer, ostensibly for working in the patrons' gardens when, in fact, they were full-time AFW staff. All were young men, and many went on to greater glory: Dale Foreman as speaker of the house and candidate for governor, Jim Waldo as a leader in environmental dispute resolution and also a candidate for governor (against Foreman!), and Bob Davidson, now CEO of the Seattle Aquarium.

When Slade Gorton decided to run for attorney general, we pushed for the idea of a united "Action Team" including Dan Evans, Slade Gorton, and Lud Kramer for secretary of state. Reed also recruited a member of the governor's urban affairs council, Art Fletcher, to run for lieutenant governor against the incumbent, "Cowboy" Johnny Cherberg. Fletcher was a member of the Pasco

City Council, the founder of a self-help cooperative there, a former professional football player, and an active Republican throughout his adult life. While he'd never been a Baptist preacher, he had the same charismatic style, soaring oratory, and cadences. Fletcher's self-help cooperative experience projected a traditional Republican message that no one should depend on government handouts. And he was black, making his nomination for a statewide office a historic event.

AFW played a significant role in the election that year, particularly in the Gorton and Fletcher races. Evans was already popular statewide, and Kramer had little opposition, but neither Gorton nor Fletcher were well known. Fletcher in particular had little in the way of organization—functionally, AFW served as Fletcher's campaign, particularly in the primary. Over the course of 1968, we rallied 2,500 people across the state to work for our candidates and built 90 percent of Gorton's campaign signs. Three members of the Action Team got elected—Gorton by a margin so narrow AFW could justly claim to have been of decisive help. Only Art Fletcher lost, a result that still rankles.

After its 1968 success, AFW drifted, doing little in 1969 for any candidate, though it never completely disappeared. Recently the idea was revived by a young Tacoma political activist, Alex Hays, though today AFW operates more as a training program for aspiring mainstream Republicans. Three AFW graduates now serve in the state legislature.

Creating AFW built on my earlier education with CHECC and was my first introduction to the nuts and bolts of partisan electoral politics. It ensured that when I considered running for something myself, I began with a base of friends, allies, and financially generous Republicans I could turn to for support.

## Setting up Shop with Slade

I did not start thinking seriously about running for King County prosecutor until the fall of 1969. But in 1968, I took the first steps toward a political career by entering government service. After I helped Slade Gorton become attorney general in 1968, he offered me a job.

During Gorton's campaign, I worked with my friend Keith Dysart to analyze the attorney general's office and recommend some improvements. Our ulterior motive was to have the new attorney general appoint me to a key leadership post. I met with Gorton on November 24, 1968, and afterward drafted a two-page memorandum covering office organization, recruitment, and beefing up the newly created office of consumer protection.

Slade ended up offering me a position ideal for building a political future: chief of consumer protection and antitrust. It made me one of three deputy attorneys general and provided great public exposure via consumer fraud alerts on the radio and suits against companies that fleeced the public. My office was in Seattle, not Olympia, making it easier to maintain connections with political allies in the city.

My colleagues at Lane Powell wished me well and were probably secretly glad to see me go, as my mind had been on politics, not billable hours, almost from my start. I settled into a corner office in Seattle's venerable Dexter Horton Building and was lucky to have excellent staff, like Kay MacDonald, who knew all the Democrats in an era when US Senators Henry "Scoop" Jackson and Warren "Maggie" Magnuson ruled Washington's congressional delegation. Slade Gorton was a wonderful boss who delegated broadly. He let me do a weekly show called *Con Man Out* on KVI radio in Seattle, on which we warned consumers of the latest frauds heading their way and solicited public input on how to improve Washington's consumer-protection statutes. And it did no harm to have my name before the public.

## Going after Carroll, King of the Courthouse

Beginning in December 1968 and continuing through 1969, my friends and I began discussing the exciting and fearsome idea of one of us running against Charles O. Carroll in the 1970 election. Doing so, we knew, would be a formidable task, for Carroll appeared impregnable.

By the late 1960s, Prosecutor Carroll stood out among courthouse politicians, both by the power of his office and the length of his tenure. Beyond his own political self-interest, Carroll also liked being a power broker in the politics of Seattle, King County, and the state. He was the closest thing King County had to a political boss. My friends and I sometimes referred to him as the second most powerful elected politician in Washington.

Carroll's power base began in his office, with around fifty deputy prosecutors plus an equal number of supporting staff. After purging the staff he inherited in 1948, he subsequently hired loyal Republicans as replacements, enhancing his power in the Republican Party. With an eye toward reelection, he chose among Republicans on the basis of ethnic identity and political connections.

Carroll made further political use of his staff after he hired them, insisting they remain politically loyal to him and work in his campaigns. Both deputies and support staff were pressured into election work—for example, making phone calls, stuffing envelopes, placing signs, and doorbelling. Months, sometimes years, before an election prosecutors would call Seattle's attorneys, often during office time, seeking names to add to Carroll's endorsement list. Allegedly, deputy prosecutors also called bar owners and tavern operators, seeking their cash donations. Carroll told one deputy, "Look, this is a political office. You want to work for me, you work for me twenty-four hours a day. I want you to work on my campaign. Donate as much money as you can to it, because when I don't have a job, you don't have a job." The "voluntary" donations were known as the "flower fund," because they were ostensibly used to buy flowers to mark office celebrations. They were a long-standing feature of all the county's political offices.

Deputies who attempted to steer their own political path did not fare well. In 1966, when future County Executive Tim Hill decided to run for the state house of representatives, he told Carroll his plans. According to Hill, Carroll said, "Hill, be out of this office by twelve," even though the deputy was in the middle of a trial. Hill had failed to clear his plans with the boss first.

Carroll's deputies also helped him after they left. Carroll usually limited prosecutors to three years' service before pushing them out the door. Carroll's imprimatur then helped former deputies secure prestigious legal jobs, judgeships, or other elected office. As his tenure lengthened, his former employees formed a substantial percentage of Seattle's judges and its local bar.

Carroll enjoyed being a kingmaker in county Republican politics. He could direct campaign contributions, both from other wealthy Republicans and from figures in the semilegal gambling world who could easily be summoned to provide quick cash. He was a popular speaker at local functions and host for fund-raisers. A rising GOP star, Carroll considered proposals to run for governor in 1956 but declined for reasons that were never clear. He later claimed it was a problem of a chronic ulcer, though he might simply have feared losing. That same year, Carroll was also invited to run against Mayor Pomeroy, a man hated by the downtown Establishment. But nothing came of that either; nor did he pursue judgeships that were probably his for the taking. Instead, he stayed in the political stronghold of the prosecutor's office, which became the base of Republican power in King County.

Opposition to Carroll did emerge from the state GOP led by Dan Evans and his allies including Slade Gorton and Joel Pritchard. But even after Evans was elected governor in 1964, Carroll kept local control through party chair Ken Rogstad, who was elected over Evans's opposition. In 1966 and 1968, the Evans faction and the Carroll-Rogstad forces waged epic battles for control of the county and state Republican Party. Each time, Evans won on the state level, while Carroll and Rogstad eked out victories in King County.

Carroll's identity as the leading figure among King County Republicans meant that in each of his elections, he started with a loyal base and organizational support his opponents were hard pressed to match. His status as Mr. Republican discouraged challenges from within the party, and until 1970, he never had a primary challenger. In 1962, Carroll beat Dan Brink by a wide margin. In 1966, no one filed against Carroll until minutes before the July 30 deadline. Democrats scrambled to find a last-minute sacrifice in young attorney Philip Meade. During the campaign, Meade made various charges against Carroll, dutifully reported on the back pages of the local newspapers. In his sole interview before the election, Carroll stated a general policy of not responding to personal attacks of any kind. He won by over one hundred thousand votes.

By 1969, Carroll had been in office for twenty-one years, gaining over time all the strength of the status quo. With the exception of some judges, nobody in King County had been in power longer. He loomed over the landscape of Seattle and King County politics by force of personality, ceaseless political activities, the power of his office, the influence of his acolytes, and sheer endurance. He stood at the pinnacle of county law enforcement but was insulated from the gritty reality of actual police practices. He had a personal campaign organization unmatched by anyone. People could not remember when he wasn't prosecutor. Whenever my friends and I discussed confronting Carroll, I felt like a rookie running back contemplating a run against the veteran linebacker Carroll, who waited, smiling, for us to try.

## King County Reforms, Reluctantly

But one factor that favored challenging Carroll was that he was reigning king of a county government that increasing numbers of people had grown to distrust and were seeking to change.

In my later campaign, one slogan that always resonated with audiences was my promise to take on the "Old Courthouse Gang." In the 1960s, Seattle's city government was derided for its stodgy passivity. But not too far away, in fact literally across the street, county government was even more dysfunctional. In Seattle, the council usurped executive powers; in King County, the merger of executive and legislative powers came baked in the pie.

Until 1969, King County functioned pursuant to state laws generally applicable to every county in Washington, from tiny Wahkiakum to mammoth King. All were governed by three commissioners nominated from separately elected districts. The commissioners decided all general matters, big and small, from zoning to hiring clerks. In King County, which topped a million people by 1970, the commissioners exercised enormous political power simply through patronage and the management of road and utility crews.

A commissioner ruled supreme in his own district. County work forces operated at his command. Road crews might, for example, put up their boss's signs during an election and take down opponents'. But the three commissioners, often politically or personally divided, found it difficult to unite or lead on long-term countywide policies.

To make the problem worse, the county charter imposed by state law divided remaining county power among eleven separately elected partisan offices, including the sheriff, the coroner, the assessor, and the county clerk. The more obscure officials depended on the political parties to round up votes in their down-ballot elections. In return, the parties benefited from opportunities for patronage. King County government was a mysterious thing. Like Seattle, the county was run by a group of semiautonomous individuals, all of whom had their own sphere of power and little overall accountability.

Improving King County government started with changing the county charter. The first unsuccessful attempt came in 1950, soon after an amendment to the state constitution allowed counties to create their own county charters, a process known as home rule. A young attorney named Jim Ellis led the effort to provide King County with its own charter and initially succeeded in getting freeholders elected to draft one. But in 1952, when the new charter reached the ballot, it lost 2–1, opposed by those who benefited from the status quo, including Prosecutor Carroll. Dismayed, Jim Ellis chose afterward to work outside of county government. He is famous in Seattle for his advocacy of a series of bond issues, collectively known as Forward Thrust, that modernized King County's patchwork of sewage districts, cleaned up Lake Washington, and also financed parks and transportation improvements. To avoid dysfunctional county government, Ellis devised an entirely new regional body, Metro, to implement his plans.

Through the rest of the fifties and into the sixties, county government changed little, although Prosecutor Carroll began to play an ever-greater role in county politics. In 1962, all three of the commissioners were Democrats. In January, however, Commissioner Howard Odell resigned, citing an ongoing criminal investigation by Carroll. Few details ever emerged about the investigation, other than that it was conducted entirely in Carroll's office using borrowed police and involved unspecified accusations of official misconduct. Democrats smelled a rat and pressured Carroll to make his accusations public, to no avail. Odell's replacement later lost to Republican Johnny O'Brien in the fall election.

In 1966, Democrats still held a 2–1 advantage among commissioners. Local Republicans were long since tired of being frozen out of county control. In a rare instance of Republicans working in harmony, the head of the state party, C. Montgomery "Gummie" Johnson, joined GOP county chair Ken Rogstad to change the balance by unseating Commissioner Scott Wallace, who was running for reelection. Johnson told local Republicans:

> We must control the Courthouse. . . . There is more patronage available through the local government at the County Courthouse than even Governor Evans controls statewide. Remember the name Scott Wallace and go after him.

In 1966, Wallace's leading opponent was John Spellman, a labor attorney who had run for mayor in 1964 and finished in fifth place. Charles O. Carroll had earlier declined to support Spellman for mayor, but in 1965 he held a meeting, including Congressman Tom Pelly, Rogstad, and Bill Boeing Jr., to persuade Spellman to run for commissioner. Spellman agreed. He later told me that after the meeting, Carroll said there was somebody he'd like Spellman to meet. Waiting outside the building was Ben Cichy, representative of the Far West Novelty Company, the front organization for King County's pinball licensees and a friend of Carroll. Carroll probably wanted Spellman to know the kind of clout he could wield.

As in 1962, Carroll used his power to influence the election. In early 1966, Carroll convened a grand jury for the purpose of investigating allegations of favoritism in contracts for renovations to the

King County Courthouse. Carroll's grand jury garnered headlines and fostered speculation regarding insider influence on county commissioners. Wallace had to endure photos showing him gamely trudging into grand jury rooms, porting boxes of documents. There's no doubt the county's process of funding capital projects had been a sloppy affair, though in the end, the jury produced only one indictment, which was immediately dismissed. But by then, Wallace's image was seriously tarnished, smoothing Spellman's win.

In the campaign itself, Carroll helped Spellman by persuading Evans's backers to support Spellman in return for Carroll staying neutral in upcoming battles over control of the party. Spellman won. Carroll and his allies now had the 2–1 Republican majority they wanted among county commissioners.

Yet Carroll ended up hoisted by his own petard. The grand jury report on courthouse operations did not taint only Scott Wallace but also county government as a whole. The municipal league joined the League of Women Voters in a renewed effort to change the charter, and John Spellman joined the Democrats to support a new election of freeholders to again rewrite the charter.

Carroll opposed a new charter in 1967, as he had in 1952. He and Rogstad ran their own slate of freeholders in the election, barely missing electing a majority. The freeholders produced a compromise charter. It replaced the three commissioners with a partisan executive and legislative council, but it retained an elected auditor and prosecutor. In 1967, the new charter passed.

In the first election in 1969, ex-governor Al Rosellini ran against King County commissioner John Spellman. By this time, Carroll had cooled on his former protégé, who had resisted some appointments urged on him by the prosecutor. But the former governor was hampered by his own reputation for ethical problems, and in the end, Spellman won without Carroll's help.

By the end of the sixties, Carroll had been on the losing end of a struggle over the reform of county government and politics. The new charter did little to directly affect the prosecutor's office, but its success demonstrated that there was a constituency ready to reform the old gray courthouse. Spellman's election also implied that Republicans could get elected countywide even without Carroll's help.

In 1969, these events made challenging Charles O. Carroll seem ever more plausible. And the prosecutor was becoming politically vulnerable for a more pointed reason: he was increasingly touched by scandal.

## CHAPTER 4

# SCANDAL

★ ★ ★ ★ ★ ★ ★ ★ ★ ★ ★ ★

While my friends and I had been busy with electoral politics in 1967 and '68, a slow-growing scandal had begun to threaten the Tolerance Policy and the police payoff system. This was a separate development from the political changes of CHECC or charter reform. Seattle's new reform politicians were more interested in replacing a stagnant group of politicians than in addressing the systematic corruption and graft that had been allowed to fester.

Instead it took a scandal to break that system—a scandal initiated by reporters and idealistic police officers. Scandal had erupted before but had never led to real change. In the late sixties, almost accidentally, scandal caught momentum and gained enough strength to threaten entrenched power, just in time for the 1970 election.

### Where It Begins—the Wilson Twins

In 1967, Seattle's greatest police scandal began like others. Dramatic stories briefly caught the public interest and then nearly faded away.

It took two *Seattle Times* reporters to get the ball rolling. John Wilson and Marshall Wilson (often called the Wilson Twins, though unrelated) were early in their careers as investigative reporters. They would break other stories over the years, but their most influential series of articles debuted in January 1967 and described a police payoff system. The stories were unprecedented in Seattle's newspaper history; the Twins appear to be the first journalists to have spent extended time interviewing bar owners about police behavior and staking out the police at night to observe what they actually did.

The *Seattle Times* published seven articles over two weeks, many on the front page. In the articles, bar owners described police shaking down a wide number of taverns, both gay bars and others, for regular cash payouts. Some bars were forced to hire off-duty police to serve as bouncers or doormen, at a wage higher than would be paid privately. If a bar owner refused to pay or hire the doormen, the police would exert pressure through systematic harassment of customers. The corruption extended to liquor board inspectors, who also took bribes, encouraged the bars to pay off the police, and helped the police enforce payoffs by threatening to suspend licenses. The articles named specific bars and specific victims. In his book, UW sociologist William Chambliss later reported rumors that the Wilsons only got permission to undertake the investigation because Chuck Carroll's *Seattle Times*–editor friend, Ross Cunningham, was out of town.

## Gay Bars—Vice or Victims?

The Wilson series had its own backstory. The Wilsons' initial interest in the story was not police corruption. Earlier, in 1966, they reported a wholly different (and to modern ears peculiar) concern—that Seattle's police were turning a blind eye to a growing "homosexual threat." The story is recounted in *Gay Seattle*, a cultural history by Gary Atkins. Gay bars and cabarets operated in Seattle for many years. Though homosexuality was not illegal per se, the legal status of same-sex dancing, drag shows, or steam houses was at least unclear. The police found excuses to harass the clientele unless paid not to.

In 1958, MacIver Wells, the owner of one of the gay bars, started complaining to the FBI about the payoffs. The FBI's interest was in whether federal politicians were on the take, but finding no evidence of that problem, the FBI did nothing else because local crimes were not their purview. Thus, one of the peculiarities of the sixties is that the local FBI were reasonably familiar with Seattle's police corruption but allowed it to continue.

In 1965, angry at both ever-increasing payoffs and the open contempt shown to him by the police when they took his money, Wells again asked the FBI to intervene. The FBI passed on word, quietly, to the Seattle police that there was a complaint. The FBI did not name the complainer, but the police figured out it was Wells based on the amounts of payoffs referenced. The police stopped asking Wells for payments. Instead, in May 1966, they started harassing him, visiting the bar frequently to check IDs, even that of Wells's eighty-year-old mother. Now even angrier, Wells contacted the *Seattle Times*.

The *Seattle Times* was more interested than the FBI in the local angle, though, initially, not more sympathetic. The Wilsons' first story, published in September 1966, inquired why the police were not cracking down sufficiently on gay bars or denying licensing. The article included quotes from the police chief decrying the influx of homosexuals to Seattle and Seattle's growing reputation as a place where the laws were soft.

This story, in itself, raised some eyebrows in city hall. Attempting to preempt accusations, Chief Ramon wrote to Mayor Braman soon after, warning the mayor of the evils attendant to places where homosexuals congregated, including the possibility some "bunco artists" might pretend to be police for the purposes of shaking bar owners down for money. Mayor Braman replied by encouraging the chief to crack down on unlicensed bars "by whatever means," including, if necessary, close surveillance to the point of harassment; doing so might discourage "these people" from coming to Seattle. In short, intentionally or not, Braman encouraged the police to keep harassing Wells.

Meanwhile, the Wilson Twins continued investigating, trying to find out why the police were so strangely lenient toward some gay bars. Wells was not making payoffs anymore, but he could point to other bars still paying. The Twins interviewed scores of bar owners and other businessmen and also surreptitiously observed a police night shift. By January, the story had changed. Gay bars were not a scourge allowed to flourish by lax police enforcement but instead were the sympathetic victims of an extortion scheme.

## The Limits of Great Journalism

The stories that ran in January 1967 laid bare major parts of the payoff system but not all of it. The Wilsons wrote only about the beat cops, not the separate payoff system run by the vice squad. Nor did they reveal what happened to the money. The Wilsons mostly talked to bar owners, who could see their money walk out the door in a paper bag but only speculate as to where it ended up.

Another weakness was that the Wilsons' best sources were the bar owners *not* making payoffs. Some, like Wells, had stopped and managed to survive. Others never paid off, like the owners of the Blue Banjo, a popular nightclub near Pioneer Square. For a time, the Banjo kept the police at bay, supported by a younger clientele largely indifferent or hostile to police as well as influential politicians who liked the Banjo. Even so, in 1966, the owners closed down the Blue Banjo and moved to Bellevue to open up a Farrell's Ice Cream Parlour. They could afford to tell the truth because they were no longer in the business. The Wilsons had less luck getting more current stories from bar owners still paying the police.

The Wilsons liked to entertain. They began and ended their series with incidents that were amusing but incidental to the larger payoff problem. The first story described several weeks of observing Seattle police officers spending their duty hours Sunday night playing poker in a bar; the bar was normally closed, but the police had a key. The cops looked more lazy than corrupt, and that initial image colored ongoing reaction to the series.

The last story contained more comedy. Chief Ramon denied being contacted by the FBI, but the Twins contradicted him, in real time, when they called an FBI agent while in Ramon's office and got the agent to admit he sent reports. The Wilsons also described a parking ticket racket going on up on Capitol Hill, where businesses would pay the police in bottles of cheap liquor to ignore customers with parking violations. One officer was described as emerging from a building staggering under the weight of the many bottles collected from businesses inside, too many to fit on his scooter.

The immediate impact of this journalistic bombshell? Surprisingly little. The *P-I* scrambled to catch up with its rival but ended up quoting only police officers complaining about the public disgrace ("My children came crying from school," said Wayne Larkin, head of the Seattle Police Officers' Guild and a vice squad officer. "My wife made me do the shopping that day.") and surveying police moonlighting practices in other cities. The *Argus* simply chalked it up to the *Seattle Times'* attempt to out-sensationalize its brash rival, the Seattle *P-I*.

Chief Ramon promised to look into the problem of cops working as tavern doormen and suspended the poker-playing officers for thirty days but denied there were systemic problems. The complaints, he said, were traceable to a single individual (presumably Wells), whom the police had investigated a long time before. He said anybody asked by the police to make a payoff should report the matter to him and denied anyone should feel reluctant to complain about the police to the police. Ramon scoffed, "Such reluctance was not the conclusion of a mature businessman."

Others simply saw the exposé as an attack on the police. The state senate passed a resolution on January 31, 1967, condemning criticisms of Seattle's police department as unfair:

> At times misfeasance or nonfeasance of duty on the part of an individual police office or several police offices is prominently and luridly treated so as to give rise to a general unwarranted feeling of public distrust and contempt for all policemen....
>
> Whereas, [a] recent instance of four violations of Seattle police regulations covering off duty conduct and of a so-far-unproved accusation of bribe solicitation by one or two members of the Seattle police force has occasioned such notoriety as to throw discredit on the entire police department of that city."

In February, a Seattle business group contacted Wayne Larkin to arrange a lunch benefit for 150 policemen to show their support of the police.

At City Hall, Mayor Braman deplored FBI involvement in local matters. He said the FBI had shown him a file regarding payoffs but claimed agents told him there was little to worry about in it, so he never read it. He emphasized to reporters that only "*very* few police officers" were involved in any kind of problem. He denied the need for a grand jury and discounted the usefulness of the city council's efficiency committee, which did have some subpoena powers, because the Wilsons were unlikely to cooperate.

But after all this deflection, Braman did take one action. Before the newspaper series ended, he appointed a citizens' committee to look into the problem. Later dubbed the Blue-Ribbon Committee, it consisted of Victor Denny, Bill Boeing Jr., and Richard Harris. Denny and Boeing were both influential Republicans and political supporters of Chuck Carroll. Denny, in fact, chaired Carroll's 1962 and 1966 campaign committees. Harris had worked for Carroll as a special deputy prosecutor on the 1966 courthouse grand jury.

Two other names were connected to the committee: Richard Auerbach and Buzz Cook. Auerbach, former head of the FBI's Seattle office, was a "special adviser" to the committee. He had accompanied Ross Cunningham to the special meeting of the municipal league board in 1962 that reversed their subpar evaluation of Carroll—the one where Cunningham boasted how Carroll's harsh methods kept Seattle free from the Mafia. The Blue-Ribbon Committee's liaison with the Seattle Police Department was Assistant Chief M. E. "Buzz" Cook, previously liaison to the Leffler committee of 1955, the one that denied any corruption. A committee less likely to embarrass the police department or Carroll could not have been created.

Whatever its membership, this committee, like previous citizens' committees, was powerless. It had no authority to subpoena documents, could not swear witnesses under oath (thus subjecting them to possible perjury), and could not indict. Nor did it conduct an independent investigation. The committee simply invited people to speak to it in confidential hearings.

Over the spring of 1967, twenty to twenty-five witnesses from Seattle's taverns and card rooms appeared before the committee to complain they were forced to pay the police for protection from harassment. The committee also heard from police officers denying any graft. The committee concluded its hearings on April 6 and published a report on April 11. As regards graft, the committee simply threw up its hands:

> The information submitted to this committee falls short
> of establishing payoffs to police officers. While a number of

statements by witnesses indicated the acceptance of payoffs by a few policemen in isolated cases, there was no substantiation or corroboration that would permit a finding by the committee as to the truth of the statements. Police officers appearing before the committee denied receiving any payoffs.

The committee disbanded, and the Wilson Twins moved on to investigate other examples of municipal mismanagement. While the Blue-Ribbon Committee operated, the police had suspended some payoffs, but they resumed demands thereafter and also ordered businesses to make retroactive payment of missed collections. In short, an apparent dead end.

But the committee did make recommendations before it closed up shop, such as ending police moonlighting at bars and suggesting officers rotate their beats no less than every two years. The shift rotation probably disrupted parts of the payoff system. Some officers not previously involved in payoffs were pressured to take them in their new locations, were reluctant to do so, and testified about it later. Ironically, in recent years, the requirement of shift rotations has been identified as a problem in reforming Seattle's current police department, as it is perhaps detrimental to long-term training of officers.

But another recommendation had a more significant and immediate impact. Committee members were perturbed by reports of lax management and understaffing in the police force, and also saw an opportunity to advocate for higher police salaries. So the committee recommended a further investigation, but one limited "to the adequacy of the number of policemen per thousand population, pay standards, and other pertinent systems which should be developed as a result of the overall study." Notably lacking was the suggestion of a further investigation of graft. Braman took up the recommendation, arranging for an audit by the International Association of Chiefs of Police (IACP), though financial wrangling regarding funding delayed the audit's start until fall 1967.

## The Audit

The IACP had been doing field studies to assist local police forces since 1935. IACP's audits focused on the nuts and bolts of management and organization, while sidestepping larger policy issues. In Seattle, the IACP began field work in September 1967, conducting extensive interviews with police at all levels. The audit ended in spring and a report eventually arrived in July 1968. It recommended numerous changes to the department's organizational structure, staffing, and patrol hours. But as regards graft, the IACP audit was nearly silent. In a section criticizing the patrol division for insufficient staffing and an artificial division between motorized and foot patrols, the IACP simply noted:

> Another problem is that a few officers, even of command rank, accept free refreshment, discounted meals, discounted services, and discounted manufactured items from commercial and business establishments. The acceptance of any service or product at prices lower than those available to the general public damages the prestige of the entire police department. The impact upon younger, more impressionable officers is tremendous. The Seattle Police Department is the highest paid department in the entire metropolitan area and it seems incongruous that its officers must accept gratuities. The practice is unprofessional and unnecessary and should unequivocally be prohibited by administrative order. Violations should be summarily dealt with.

No other part of the report mentioned graft. The most careful reader of the report would have no idea the Seattle Police Department was systematically extorting substantial cash payoffs from businesses. The report made no reference to the Wilson Twins' articles.

The IACP report is a long, detailed, and boring document. It might have mostly gathered dust. But, at least indirectly, the audit and report put in motion significant changes.

First, while doing their audit, IACP investigators did question police regarding graft and heard from several, such as high-ranking officer David Jessup, that payoffs were happening. Although the IACP report made no mention of the payoff system as such, it provided political leadership in Seattle with an unofficial report detailing some of what they had learned, alerting senior officers that by continuing the system, they were running the risk of exposure.

But the IACP's principal effect was more indirect. The report's chief recommendation for organizational change was to change the role of the assistant police chief, who until then was the chief's single gatekeeper and received reports formally and informally from all other departments. The report recommended replacing one assistant chief with several—one for each department, all reporting directly to the chief.

At the time, the assistant chief was Buzz Cook. It was one of the quirks of the old system that the assistant chief, in addition to receiving reports from other departments, was also directly in charge of the patrol division, where the payoffs chiefly originated before funneling upward. This ensured that Cook could both monitor payoffs and receive a direct share. Like previous assistant chiefs, Cook was principally responsible for maintaining the payoff system, much more so than the police chief. (The payoff system may have affected other aspects of police organization. A police officer told me that at that time, there were no lieutenants in Precinct One—the downtown precinct—because payoffs were passed up by grade levels. By eliminating the lieutenant layer, above patrolmen and sergeants, more police leadership guaranteed more money for the higher-ups.)

City hall did implement the recommended reorganization, reducing Cook to just one of four assistant chiefs. The others, named after consulting with the IACP, were Tony Gustin, Eugene Corr, and George Fuller. After the change, Cook lost direct connections to both the patrol divisions and the vice squad—the former being headed by Fuller, the latter by Gustin.

The change introduced reformers into police leadership. Of the four new assistant chiefs, at least two, Corr and Gustin, had never taken payoffs. Fuller's involvement had been relatively minimal, though sufficient for Cook and others to think he could be trusted. As it turned out, though, Fuller wanted reform and soon started gathering evidence of payoffs for possible later use.

More important, though, was the rise of Tony Gustin. He had a reputation in the department, noted by the IACP, for hard work and a clean record. Gustin, who is still alive as of this writing, is brave, idealistic, independent, abrasive, and, at heart, a crusader.

But while Gustin was starting to reorganize the vice squad, another development rocked Seattle. Seattle once had two great newspapers, neither of which liked to be outdone. In 1968, the *Post-Intelligencer* did its own stakeout and got its own scoop.

## Cichy and Carroll, Together Tonight

The Wilson Twins focused on the lowest and most embittered level of the corrupt system—the tavern owners and card room operators paying each month to keep their businesses open. But in 1968, the *P-I* took a different path by attempting to identify the highest level.

In August 1968, the *P-I* put on its front page the most important photo it may have ever published, a shadowy picture of a man standing at the entry of a house on north Capitol Hill. The man was Ben Cichy, and the house belonged to Charles O. Carroll. *P-I* reporters

# Pinball King Is Tailed to Home Of Prosecutor

*In this murky photo taken August 21, 1968, Carroll and Cichy are discernable beyond the prosecutor's idling county Pontiac.*

had observed Cichy meet with Carroll three times in three months, on about the same date, each time arriving with a briefcase and staying about an hour.

Ben Cichy, a native Seattleite, was in his sixties. He was reasonably well known in Seattle's established circles; he lived on Yarrow Point, owned a yacht, and belonged to some clubs. But his real notoriety was his occupation. He was the president of the Far West Novelty Company, which held King County's sole license to lease pinball machines, a business that raked in millions, and for which privilege Far West paid the county $20,000 each year. Cichy was the most public face of Seattle's tolerated gambling industry. The pictures of Carroll and Cichy together, meeting on a regular basis, awakened the unavoidable suspicion that perhaps Carroll was not just a passive observer of Seattle's commercial vice, but a participant and beneficiary.

Within days, Carroll was also the target of *Seattle* magazine. Carroll's unflattering mug shot graced the front cover of *Seattle*'s August 1968 edition, under the headline "Remove Charles Carroll." The story inside sprawled over many pages and spent time on Carroll's anger issues and his difficulties with minorities. But the story's real focus was Carroll's passivity with respect to illegal gambling and his tacit support of the Tolerance Policy. The appearance of this article soon after the *P-I* photographs was no coincidence, the *P-I* and *Seattle* had been collaborating on the idea of targeting Carroll.

In the brouhaha following the photos, Carroll further damaged his reputation by refusing to respond to press inquiries. As it happened, regardless of what else was going on, he and Cichy were longtime friends. The two went to the same high school and yachted together on the Puget Sound. But instead of trying to explain away the association, Carroll stonewalled the press, even the *Times*.

Sensational as they were, the photos and the articles provided no direct proof that either Carroll or Cichy were corrupt. Cichy was not a criminal, and his meeting with Carroll was not, in itself, a criminal act. The *P-I* simply speculated as to why a prosecutor and a pinball operator might meet regularly at night. *Seattle* accused Carroll of bad temper, partisan politics, and indifference to prosecuting commercial vice but admitted it could not provide evidence of actual malfeasance. Yet the stories' content mattered less than the nighttime photo and the magazine cover. The *P-I* picture implied a story even more startling than the Wilsons' thousands of

Seattle *magazine makes its sentiments clear in a cover*
*article that runs the same month the* P-I *runs its exposé.*

words, and raised a question to which Carroll refused to provide
an answer. The *Seattle* cover hammered home the possibility that
Carroll finally was politically vulnerable.

The story had an immediate impact, publicly and behind the
scenes. Within a day or two of the story, Buzz Cook sent word out
to other police to shut down the payoff system. Payoffs had been
suspended before—for example, after MacIver Wells complained to
the FBI and during the Blue-Ribbon Committee investigation. But
after a hiatus, payoffs had always returned. This time, the suspension
proved more enduring. Of course, linking the end of the payoffs to

the Cichy-Carroll photograph is speculative. Cook never admitted a connection. But the timing would otherwise be an odd coincidence.

Not that the payoff system completely shut down that August. Bingo parlors, for example, continued to make large dollar payoffs through 1968 and into 1969. And there are scattered reports of police demanding cash right through 1969. In Ross Anderson's "Seattle Confidential," published in *Seattle Metropolitan* magazine, he includes this sourceless vignette: "A cop who joined the force in 1969 recalls walking First Avenue with his veteran partner. The old bull found two shots of whiskey waiting for him at each bar and tossed down both. Rounding the corner onto Pike Street, he collects a couple cigars and an envelope full of cash. The young rookie had no choice but to tag along." Reports also surfaced in the summer of 1970 that some officers had briefly attempted to revive payoffs.

But payoffs to ordinary beat patrolmen mostly ended in August 1968, a relief to bar owners and to some cops. There were a large number of new hires appearing in the force at the time, and they had a chance to begin in a system where payoffs were no longer part of the daily work.

The Cichy-Carroll photo had another, more public impact. The summer of 1968 was the middle of an election year, for both president and governor. The Cichy photograph landed in hot political waters, making quite a splash.

## Hot Uncooked Potato

That August, three men were actively running for Washington governor. Dan Evans wanted reelection after a successful first term. He was a Republican but led a moderate faction in open conflict with Carroll's conservatives. John J. O'Connell was the state's attorney general and a Democrat. Competing with O'Connell in the Democratic primary was Martin Durkan Sr., a state senator with substantial clout.

Within a day of the photos being published, O'Connell called for an investigation. Carroll was not a political ally of Governor Evans, but they were both Republicans, making Carroll a natural target for O'Connell. Besides, O'Connell would benefit from headlines of him actively investigating corruption. Unfortunately for O'Connell, this lunge for glory was complicated by state law, which required the attorney general to get permission from Evans to start an investigation.

Evans criticized Carroll's stonewalling but was reluctant to take up the matter. Yet the *P-I*, led by its relentless editor Lou Guzzo, would not let him duck, pushing Evans to make his own investigation.

While O'Connell and Evans argued over whether Carroll would be investigated, and by whom, Senator Durkan saw an opportunity to upstage his Democratic rival. Durkan initiated plans to hold committee hearings on corruption issues. He planned the hearings in Seattle itself, maximizing public interest and journalistic coverage.

Resolving the conflict between these three politicians seeking the governor's office proved complicated. Without waiting for Evans's say so, O'Connell began staffing an investigation, including Assistant Attorney General David Boerner, who later became chief of my criminal division. Another important hire was a nonlawyer, Reg Bruce, a one-man investigative team who started interviewing Pioneer Square bar owners and gambling operators, looking for evidence.

Meanwhile, within a week of the Cichy photo, Evans bowed to *P-I* pressure and met with Carroll, twice. The first was a forty-five-minute session at the governor's Seattle Center office, behind closed doors, outside of which journalists gathered and after which little was said. The second meeting came a few days later, on a Sunday evening at Carroll's house on Capitol Hill. Evans went there alone to review Carroll's financial accounts privately.

In a later interview, Evans admitted acute discomfort regarding this Sunday visit and the task of rummaging through Carroll's private bank statements and financial accounts. "I felt like a financial voyeur," he told me later. Evans also understood his limitations; he was not an accountant and didn't know whether the records he saw were complete. Still, as he said later, the numbers all seemed to match up with Carroll's income from his salary and his inheritances. There was no clear evidence, such as regular cash deposits, indicating bribes. Evans did recall being impressed Carroll was doing so well financially.

Evans duly relayed to the press he had found nothing untoward, though again he criticized Carroll's refusal to explain his meetings with Cichy. Evans said further investigation, if necessary, should be left to King County Superior Court judges, who had the statutory power to call a grand jury. He suggested anyone who had information, such as O'Connell, should give it to the judges. Evans's attitude toward the O'Connell investigation had hardened, and from then on, he would tell the press it was little but a naked political ploy.

For his part, O'Connell publicly stated his reluctance to provide the judges with the information he'd gathered, calling it an "uncooked potato." He said a grand jury was premature until after an investigation produced more facts. Defying Evans, he kept his investigation going, relying, he said, on the attorney general's inherent powers.

As for Durkan, his attempt to grab headlines fizzled. He arranged for a hearing at the Olympic Hotel, a convenient locale for any interested journalist. But Durkan found it difficult to get anyone to appear, and he had no subpoena powers. Carroll, for one, politely declined an invitation. Durkan ended up postponing his hearings, first until after the primary and then, after being defeated, indefinitely.

That fall, Evans and O'Connell continued to duel in the papers, each touting his own approach to the investigation. But O'Connell's investigation of gambling in Seattle was eventually derailed by his own problems with gambling in Nevada. In mid-October, the Wilson Twins made new headlines in the *Times* by printing copies of a check that appeared to show O'Connell had set up a $10,000 line of credit at a Las Vegas hotel in 1965. They also reported O'Connell cashing a $12,625 check representing gambling winnings. At a minimum, the reports made it clear that O'Connell played for fairly high stakes in Las Vegas. Also, though, was the innuendo that Vegas gamblers could do O'Connell favors by forgiving debts and persuading hotel staff to cover up embarrassing stories.

O'Connell could only respond that yes, he liked to gamble, but it was legal in Nevada. He provided the press with a six-thousand-word white paper accusing the Evans campaign of leaking the report to the press and accusing both Evans and the *Seattle Times* of colluding in an attempt to stop his investigation of vice. How, he demanded, could the *Times* have gotten the copies of checks if somebody in Las Vegas had not wanted to taint him? Both then and now, Evans denies being the source, though suspicions have always abounded that somebody in the Evans campaign was behind the leak.

In any case, the story probably had an effect. Although O'Connell accused Evans of obstructing the vice investigation, O'Connell's own association with high-stakes gambling put him on the defensive, never a good place for a politician. O'Connell was trailing prior to the exposé, but afterward his standing sank further. He ended up losing in November.

As for the King County Superior Court, in the fall of 1968, they issued an invitation to the public, accompanied by a post office box number, asking for any "information persons might have regarding the break-down of law enforcement in King County." Unsurprisingly, this drew little response.

The judges' executive committee had several meetings on the subject that fall, and David Boerner remembers going to one with O'Connell. The judges were simply unimpressed with any of it, thinking that the supposed scandal was just a question of politics and that gambling tolerance was an open secret. Many, in addition, were former deputy prosecutors and Carroll supporters.

After O'Connell was defeated in November, he sent the judges the results of his investigation. The judges briefly considered the accumulated information and voted, unanimously, that there wasn't enough evidence to warrant a grand jury. Later, Washington Supreme Court justice Robert Utter, who was a King County Superior Court judge in 1968, did not recall it ever being seriously discussed.

Thus, by the end of 1968, the scandal caused by the *P-I*'s Cichy-Carroll photos had apparently petered out—just as the Wilson Twins' 1967 exposé had—due to an ineffectual investigation and no public action. But there were lingering long-term effects.

The Wilson Twins had exposed the rancid details of police payoffs. But the more subtle corruption of the Tolerance Policy, involving mayoral policy, council ordinances, and the activities of the city's license committee, had always been a separate issue. Payoffs in the form of license fees, taxes, and campaign contributions were technically legitimate. But the Cichy photograph turned gambling tolerance itself into something questionable. It raised the question of how far Seattle's gamblers were going to ensure favorable treatment. Did Cichy's briefcases contain cash, from campaign contributions or otherwise? To a growing part of the population, Seattle's gambling culture became identified, inherently, as a corrupting influence at all levels of law enforcement.

The Cichy photographs also irredeemably tarnished Carroll's image. He had been criticized before for passivity toward commercial vice, but he had never been directly implicated in its operations.

Finally, and most concretely, the Cichy photograph put David Boerner and Reg Bruce into motion. O'Connell's team began the type of investigative police work needed for later criminal action. Like reporters and citizens' committees, Bruce listened to bar owners' complaints and talked to police. But Bruce was working toward a more long-term goal than an article or committee report; he was doing the systematic work needed to put together a criminal case. Bruce left the attorney general's office that fall, but Boerner remained, following leads, making connections, and preserving the files and contacts needed if someone wanted to pick up the baton.

Still, in all, 1967 and 1968 were simply prologue. It was not until 1969 that the balls really started rolling. Three figures in particular stand out that year, men of different temperaments but similar stubbornness. Moving in parallel, the headstrong Tony Gustin and the more cerebral Slade Gorton both acted decisively during 1969. Between them, they set the stage for the arrival of a third man, Stan Pitkin, to finally and fully expose a corrupt police department.

## Rogue Cop—David Jessup

The story of scandals in 1967 and 1968 would be incomplete without a tip of the hat to an officer who tried, single-handedly, to end police payoffs—an effort whose methods were murky and whose results were inconclusive but was admirable nonetheless, particularly given the eventual price paid.

In 1967, David Jessup was a rising star in the department, but one increasingly disturbed by the graft he observed. A crystallizing incident came in 1967, when two beat cops put the squeeze on Richard Murray, who owned the Stage Door Tavern. Murray complained to City Councilmember Floyd Miller, Mayoral Assistant Bob Lavoie, and Chief Ramon. Ramon appeared to take it seriously, giving Murray fifty dollars in marked money and posting Jessup and another cop on the stakeout to observe the handover. The next day, the beat cops never showed up, and Ramon called Mayor Braman to tell him the whole thing had been a waste of time. But Jessup heard that Ramon had let Assistant Chief Cook know about the stakeout, and Cook told the officers to lay off.

In late 1967, Jessup decided to approach Ed Devine, another mayoral assistant, and offer to do an investigation from the inside. The mayor's office put him off. On his own, Jessup then spent months trying to gather evidence about the payoffs. To win the trust of the other officers, Jessup took payoff money himself, totaling $1,900. By August 1968, Jessup had enough evidence, he thought, to go back to the mayor's office. Braman responded by putting him in charge of a task force to address citizen complaints. At the same time, Braman told Jessup he did not want to hear much more about payoffs and was more interested in the riots then occurring in the Central District. Frustrated, Jessup quit a week later, on August 20, and took his concerns to Ramon. Ramon proved to be no more help, and at this point Jessup gave up, saving his evidence for later corruption trials.

Jessup's story illustrates the difficulties honest cops faced at the time. A Seattle police officer could keep his own hands clean but subsequently would have little concrete information to report about graft, because those who ran the system would ensure he never observed it. An officer who wanted to confront and change the system, without real support from a mayor or chief, needed evidence, which was hard to obtain without taking payoffs himself. And taking money is always suspect. Did Jessup really take payoffs to gather evidence? Or did he do it to advance his career by demonstrating himself as trustworthy to the police hierarchy, and perhaps to line his pockets? Did his motive for taking the money even matter when he had no one's permission to break the law but his own?

Jessup's single-handed attempt to uncover police corruption got no public notice at the time. But later he claimed it did produce one good result. Buzz Cook sent the word out to the beat cops to stop taking payoffs within a day of Jessup going to Chief Ramon with evidence of graft. Jessup said that he, not the Carroll-Cichy photo in the *P-I*, was responsible for Cook's decision to suspend payoffs in August 1968. From this distance, with little other information available, it's difficult to say which of these two events, if not both, put graft on its permanent hiatus. No one in a position to know for sure, Cook or otherwise, ever explained the decision.

## Gorton Clears the Ground

In 1968, Slade Gorton won the election for attorney general, running as a Republican reformer, like Evans. His platform included changing Washington's blanket ban on gambling to distinguish between its minor forms and the larger, more commercial ventures. During the campaign, he earned Carroll's enmity. Gorton's opponent, the conservative Democrat John McCutcheon, claimed to stand for "law 'n' order." Gorton remarked those concerned with law and order should look at the "mess" in King County. Carroll was not amused, and he and Rogstad arranged for use of a party mailing list to send word out to Republican precinct committee members and others in the party that it was OK to vote against Gorton. In contrast to Evans's comfortable victory, Gorton's eventual winning margin in 1968 was razor thin.

When Gorton arrived in office, he inherited the remains of O'Connell's investigative team and their files. And within a few days, Gorton took his first big step. David Boerner was a Democrat, who had worked for a Democrat. He was pretty sure Gorton would be putting his own people into the office, and when Gorton asked to meet with him, Boerner anticipated being released. Instead, Gorton asked him what he was working on. Boerner told Gorton he was investigating police corruption in Seattle. Surprising Boerner, Gorton told him to continue. There was only one rule, said Gorton: I do the politics. Thus, O'Connell's investigation would continue. Boerner and later Reg Bruce, who returned to the office, spent 1969 trying to put the pieces together.

Bruce and Boerner could not, on their own, come up with enough evidence to prove particular officers guilty of crimes. They were hampered in part by a problem of jurisdiction—in Washington, county prosecutors, not the attorney general, decide who to prosecute for state crimes. And though they heard stories, they lacked documentation to prove payoffs went higher than beat cops. So, in July 1969, Gorton published an official report following up on O'Connell's investigation, finding insufficient evidence for indictments but criticizing Carroll for failing to meet with the press. At the same time, Gorton wrote to Carroll privately, encouraging him to investigate the evidence that had been uncovered concerning payoffs. Carroll ignored him. After the report, Bruce and Boerner continued to work on rounding up evidence and contacts, including holding regular meetings with the intrepid Tony Gustin, a much more receptive audience than Carroll.

Meanwhile, Gorton took another big step by taking on the tangled problem of Washington's gambling laws. Initially he pushed for legislation to clarify what types of gambling would or would not be allowed in Washington, trying to carve out a place for small-scale bingo games or lotteries by valid nonprofits or churches. But that bill did not pass, as it was opposed by Washington's gambling interests, who did not want a legal distinction between large- and small-scale gambling.

Undeterred, in April 1969, Gorton cut through the legal ambiguity surrounding gambling tolerance by issuing a legal opinion. It stated pinball machines, card rooms, sports cards, bingo games, and lotteries were all illegal, regardless of the gambling licenses issued by Seattle and other cities. An attorney general's opinion has no formal legal effect—it is literally just an opinion. But it's an opinion that carries weight, and it put Washington's cities on the defensive, encouraging many to abandon local tolerance policies.

In King County, the showdown occurred in the summer of 1969. Newly elected King County Executive John Spellman announced he intended to let licenses for some pinball machines expire, and perhaps also the county's card room licenses. Realistically, the county gained remarkably little legitimate revenue from its licenses, only $23,800 for the year. Most of that was a single $20,000 fee paid by the holder of the county's only master pinball license, the Far West Novelty Company, Ben Cichy's outfit. Later in July, the county council passed a new licensing ordinance (crafted and pushed by Councilmember Ed Heavey, soon to be a candidate for prosecutor) without repealing the old ordinance. This left matters still legally confused (perhaps intentionally), so Spellman simply announced the county would stop providing licenses. Thus ended the Tolerance Policy, at least in the county.

In Seattle there was a new mayor, Floyd Miller, appointed when Dorm Braman left office in early 1969 to work for the Nixon administration. Miller reacted to Gorton's opinion by instructing Ramon to simply enforce all the gambling laws, regardless of city licensing, the same tactic used by Gordon Clinton five years earlier. As happened before, the council then had to decide whether to persist in requiring gambling licenses even if they were theoretically of no protection against arrest.

Some of the older members of the council, particularly Charles M. "Streetcar Charlie" Carroll, the chair of the licensing committee, favored drafting a new Tolerance Policy, more or less in defiance of Gorton's opinion. However, the new CHECC-backed members pushed to end licensing and got a majority of the council to support them. On July 18, the council voted to end all licensing of multiple-coin pinball machines and of card rooms (with Streetcar Charlie Carroll dissenting). For nearly fifty years, Seattle had licensed illegal gambling for the money and for the goal of local control. Those days were over.

And they did not come back, though not for lack of trying by the gambling industry. A couple of councilmembers, George Cooley and Liem Tuai, reported being contacted by unnamed people promising money if licensing was reinstated. Rumors flew that gambling interests would fund candidates running in the fall election for mayor and the four council positions coming open. But the days when gambling money could control the council were coming to an end. None of the candidates would openly admit to accepting the support.

Gambling advocates did score one victory in 1969, when Vice Squad Police Officer Wayne Larkin beat City Councilmember Don Wright. But even together, Larkin and Streetcar Charlie Carroll could not revive the policy in the face of the opposition from the rest of the council and Seattle's new mayor, Wes Uhlman.

Gorton played a supporting role to Governor Evans in one more major change in 1969. Newly elected President Richard Nixon would be appointing a new US attorney for Washington's Western District. Evans and Gorton were impressed with Stan Pitkin, the young Whatcom County prosecuting attorney. Pitkin had led reform efforts in his own county and made a well-regarded speech at a prosecutors' conference on the issue of gambling toleration. It did not hurt that Pitkin had strongly supported Evans in 1968.

Normally, the White House would take the advice of a senior federal legislator regarding a federal appointment. In the absence of Republican senators, this meant Seattle Congressman Tom Pelly. In February, Evans told Pelly he wanted Pitkin. Pelly agreed, after getting a promise Pitkin would not run for Pelly's seat later. But Pelly had failed to clear the choice with Chuck Carroll.

Carroll preferred one of his ex-deputies, Joel Rindal, for the position. Carroll persuaded Pelly to change his recommendation and put Rindal's name before Nixon. Local Republican notables in Carroll's camp flew to Washington DC to make the pitch for Rindal. Pelly even threatened Nixon that he would withhold his vote on a pending antiballistic missile system if Rindal wasn't appointed.

But the Evans-Gorton contingent fought back. The choice of a US attorney was significant. Although gambling laws were mostly state created, the transportation of gambling equipment was a federal felony. An aggressive US attorney could prosecute such a case, as Brock Adams had in 1962. The head of the state Republican Party, Montgomery "Gummie" Johnson, an Evans ally, flew to DC to tell White House advisers Richard Kleindienst and John Ehrlichman, an attorney from Seattle, that it would not be a good idea to appoint Rindal, at the time an attorney for Far West Novelty Company. Gummie buttressed his argument by noting Pelly hadn't supported Nixon in the 1968 Republican primaries. In the end, the White House nominated Pitkin, and Congress confirmed him in the summer of 1969. Pitkin took office that fall, and one of his first visitors was Slade Gorton, carrying with him a year's worth of investigation by Boerner and Bruce into the activities of Seattle's police department.

## The Great Bingo Raid

In the fall of 1969, Gustin finally made his move. The biggest hurdle to all previous investigations had been the thin blue line—the refusal of police officers to investigate wrongdoing or take any efforts to expose the payoffs that might implicate fellow officers. In 1969, though, Tony Gustin broke that line.

Gustin is famous in Seattle's police history, a man of strong opinions and personal integrity coupled with a devious mind.

Mayor Uhlman provided me with an example of Gustin playing the game of politics. Gustin paid a visit to Uhlman at his campaign headquarters while Uhlman was running for mayor in the fall of 1969. In private, Gustin told Uhlman a woman had accused Uhlman of complicity in murder. Gustin said he had come by to let Uhlman know Gustin thought the woman was crazy and would not be making her accusations public. And, in fact, the woman was later declared insane and committed. The unspoken predicate, that Gustin was doing Uhlman a significant favor by keeping this all quiet right before the election, was left unspoken.

Gustin managed to rise through the ranks without participating in the payoffs, and once in a position of power as assistant chief, he immediately began making plans to expose the corruption. He began 1969 by transferring the entire existing vice squad to other positions. The payoff system of the time funneled money to two parallel sets of officers: the beat cops for various districts, mostly downtown; and the vice squad, whose jurisdiction was citywide. There's some evidence the vice squad officers were in overall control, advising other officers what prices to set. (One of these vice squad officers was Wayne Larkin, who ran for city council in 1969. Larkin always cheerfully denied having anything to do with payoffs. But someone knowledgeable about municipal politics of the time laughingly referred to him and his partner as the team of Parkin and

Larkin, known for taking money up and down First Avenue.) Gustin's reforms did not go unnoticed. At some point in January 1969, one of his fellow officers let Gustin know $40,000 was available if he went easy on enforcing gambling laws. Gustin turned the money down. Not long after, someone fired a bullet through his window.

Gustin assembled a team of police officers with clean records to replace the previous vice squad and began planning a raid. Over the summer of 1969, the team practiced by making arrests at clubs primarily patronized by blacks in the Central District, which were of less interest to the police establishment.

Gustin was not acting alone. David Boerner and Reg Bruce in the attorney general's office met with him weekly to discuss strategy and share information, often over coffee in the county's administration building. Bruce in particular had informants who could indicate where usable evidence could be found. Gustin also enlisted the support of sympathetic city councilmembers. Shortly after Don Wright took office in spring 1969 (replacing Floyd Miller), Gustin briefed Wright regarding the influence of gambling money.

At the end of summer, Gustin prepared for his most important raid. He took steps to disguise his tracks, including leaving fake memos on his desk to throw off any other police officers who might be looking through his papers. And then on a damp Wednesday afternoon, September 24, Gustin led a squad of thirty-four officers to the Lifeline Club bingo parlor at the Pike Place Market. They went up the stairs behind DeLaurenti Specialty Food and Wine and burst in on a room containing eighty-six startled players, mostly elderly women taking a break from shopping at the Bon Marché.

The market's Lifeline Club was one of three such operations managed by seventy-two-year-old Charles Berger. Ostensibly nonprofits benefiting disabled alcoholics, in reality the operations were large-scale gambling enterprises, grossing many hundreds of thousands and paying Charles Berger a salary of over $100,000.

The bingo clubs could generate such profits in part because they did not spend much on prizes; according to income tax returns, prizes amounted to $2,900 for all of 1968. Berger's bingo parlors also thrived through fraud. The Lifeline, like other bingo parlors of the time, sold bingo cards that were impossible to fill and planted marks in the audience to claim the large prizes of $500 before anybody else could.

The customers were not the target of the raid on September 24. They were let off with a citation, though some of the staff were kept overnight in jail. Gustin's real target was records, carefully kept by Berger, listing his costs and expenses. Among the expenses was $3,000 Berger paid each month to local nightclub owner Frank Colacurcio to protect against police harassment. (In later testimony, Berger stated he had initially paid only $2,000 per month, but it became $3,000 after police pressured him to open up another bingo parlor on the other side of Pike Street; Pike Street divided two police beats, and the police previously left out wanted part of

*Charlie Berger at the Lifeline Club bingo parlor over the Pike Place Market while being raided by Tony Gustin and vice squad.*

the action.) Also intriguing was a list of campaign contributions made to a variety of local politicians. Effectively, Gustin had executed an armed subpoena for documents, which he took back to police headquarters for examination. Rick Anderson, in *Seattle Vice*, reported attempts were made in the department to steal the records from Gustin after the raid, and Gustin said later that some evidence disappeared from the evidence room. But Gustin and his handpicked team managed to keep most of his haul intact.

## The Palace Guard Leads a Palace Revolt

The Lifeline Club raid made the police chief, Frank Ramon, very unhappy. He ordered the immediate release of Charles Berger (and gave Berger back his gun), told reporters there would be no more such raids, and cut off Gustin's funds for further investigations. Then he left town for a convention in Florida, leaving Buzz Cook in charge. (It was about this time that Al Rosellini, the ex-governor, called Mayor Miller and Chief Ramon to find out what was going on and encourage the reopening of the Lifeline Club.)

When Ramon returned two weeks later, he faced trouble from a different direction. In the interim, Councilmember Don Wright told the press of his conversations with Gustin, including Gustin's mention of a $40,000 bribe offer. Tim Hill and others called for a city council investigation. Mayor Miller discounted the need for such a step but was upset Ramon never told him about the bribe attempt.

At the same time, Ramon also confronted an angry Tony Gustin. Gustin and Ramon had been in conflict for months, and for Gustin, Ramon's reaction to the Lifeline raid—obstructing further investigations and disregarding payoff records—was the last straw. Gustin told two other assistant chiefs, Eugene Corr and George Fuller, that he was prepared to resign or seek demotion to captain. (As captain,

Gustin would be protected by civil service rules and not otherwise subject to dismissal.) Instead, Fuller and Corr told Gustin they would join him in confronting Ramon, demanding Ramon either resign or face their joint resignation or demotion. The press quickly dubbed this the "Palace Revolt" and the three assistant chiefs the "Palace Guard." It may have been the first time in Seattle Police Department history that the senior leadership of the department pushed for reform against the will of the police chief.

On Monday, October 6, Gustin, Corr, and Fuller met with Ramon and, in a stormy meeting, accused him of covering up corruption. The revolt became public when the three assistant chiefs followed up by marching to the city council and briefing councilmembers on their concerns and their dissatisfaction with Ramon.

*George Fuller, Eugene Corr, and Tony Gustin, the "Palace Guard," in a cropped and marked up P-I photo.*

On October 8, Mayor Miller fired Ramon, just weeks before a new mayor, Wes Uhlman, would take office.

All this time, the Lifeline bingo raid itself had dropped out of the press because of the turmoil about the $40,000 bribe and the Palace Revolt. But Gustin had been making edited versions of Berger's records available to the press, and on the evening of October 8, the same day as Ramon's resignation, Don McGaffin of KOMO TV news ran a story like Seattle had never seen. McGaffin had been working on a related story regarding the police department for an entire year, interviewing nearly one-third of the 1,100-member police force. He found a department demoralized and split by generations, with many of the newer members upset at the pressure to take payoffs. This story probably put him in contact with Gustin, who shared the bingo records. That October 8, McGaffin described to his audience how gambling had expanded beyond a game "played by gray-haired little ladies in church basements for prizes such as electric blankets or toasters" and become a huge commercial gambling operation. McGaffin drew a connection between the Lifeline raid and a problematic police leadership by pointing out Ramon had gotten Berger released immediately.

*KOMO TV's Don McGaffin held up this Charlie Berger check in a 1969 broadcast on gambling.*

And, dramatically, McGaffin showed his audience copies of checks written by Berger to various local politicians, stating:

> We do not suggest that each of these people either solicited the money, performed any services for it—or even knew this money had flown into their campaign funds. But we do suggest that any elected official who takes money from bingo or gambling sources must expect that he will be asked to explain.

For the next few days, reporters from the daily papers made the bingo raid records their front page story, competing with the continuing fallout of Ramon's resignation. The press detailed the many contributions Berger made to numerous local politicians, including Seattle City Councilmember Charles M. Carroll, King County sheriff Jack Porter, Washington State Representative Ed Heavey, Washington State Senator Gordon Walgren, US Congressman Brock Adams, and many others. As some people noted, all of the politicians named were Democrats. Berger said he'd always been a strong Democrat himself. All denied knowing anything other than that a nonprofit charity running an innocent bingo game had generously helped out their campaigns. Senator Walgren, from Kitsap County, complained bitterly to the press that Gustin's raid was an abuse of power and that Gustin's real purpose was not to crack down on gambling but to embarrass politicians. He convened a meeting of his committee for the ostensible purpose of investigating gambling in Seattle but actually to condemn Gustin's actions. However, he got little support from his fellow legislators.

As for Charles Berger, he was not having a good autumn. Shortly after the raid, two mysterious hooded men attacked him, stabbing him in the stomach, and from August to October 1969, his house was burglarized four times by persons unknown. But Berger did have one bit of luck. Immediately after the raid, Prosecutor Carroll decided the evidence captured only supported charges of possession of gambling equipment, a gross misdemeanor, instead of the felony gambling charges the police thought were warranted. When police complained to the press, Chief Criminal Deputy Prosecutor Bill Kinzel, on behalf of Carroll, blamed Chief Ramon for the charging decision.

Like the Carroll-Cichy photographs, the Lifeline Club raid was a spectacular event whose real effects were more long term than immediate. Berger's campaign contributions embarrassed a lot of politicians but were not illegal. Most of the politicians involved, like Ed Heavey, immediately disassociated themselves from Berger and denied any knowledge of his activities. No one in the police department or prosecutor's office used Berger's record of police payoffs to start an investigation. If they had, because he was charged only with misdemeanors, Berger would have faced little pressure to testify.

The raid did cause the removal of Chief Ramon. His first replacement was Buzz Cook, who then quit after Mayor Miller told him he would not be allowed to fire Gustin, Fuller, or Corr. At that point, one of Cook's deputies, Frank Moore, who had his own connections to the payoff system, took his place as acting chief. Everyone waited for the fall election to see what a new mayor would do.

But though the raid and the Palace Revolt did not immediately change the system, they did have a strong effect on the public. It revived the feeling of the previous year, after the Cichy-Carroll photo, that there was something fundamentally rotten about Seattle politics. In 1969, newly elected mayor Wes Uhlman and King County Executive John Spellman came from outside the system and escaped the taint. But there was another powerful local politician who had been in office for over twenty years: King County Prosecutor Charles O. Carroll.

Above all, the Lifeline Club raid, unlike the Cichy-Carroll photo, came when the attorney general was Slade Gorton, not John O'Connell. Gorton's deputies had been helping Gustin all along, Evans fully supported Gorton, and Gorton was not running for election. Gorton promised the press he would follow up on the Lifeline revelations. For one thing, he said, he had an appointment to talk to new US Attorney Stan Pitkin at the latter's investiture in October.

## One More Thing

Another enduring mystery of this era stems from an event that took place on May 31, 1969. That morning, around eleven or eleven thirty, Ben Cichy walked across his lawn to work on his yacht, which was moored at the dock of his expensive home on Yarrow Point. His wife then took a nap, woke up, and could not find Cichy. She started calling those he was supposed to see that day, including the attorney for the Far West Novelty Company, Joel Rindal, who Carroll was then touting for US attorney. A rookie deputy sheriff arrived around seven that night to find already present Rindal and a King County deputy prosecutor, Fred Yeatts, with whom Cichy had been supposed to meet at two that afternoon. The rookie deputy called divers, who quickly found Cichy's body in five feet of water near the dock. As per the officer's later report, Cichy had his glasses and slippers on, and was floating in a sitting position, as if he were in a chair, with a smile on his face. The officer thought he did not look like somebody who had fallen off a dock into the lake; if he had, the glasses would have been knocked off.

An autopsy of Cichy was to be performed the next day, on the weekend, in the presence of the police as called for by the law. But the chief medical examiner, then on vacation on Whidbey Island, told the coroner's office to stop the autopsy and wait for him to come back. The examiner, Gayle Wilson, was also Chuck Carroll's brother-in-law. Wilson arrived Monday morning, did the autopsy himself, without witnesses, and declared the cause of death to be drowning following a heart attack.

And that, to this day, is what is known for sure about the death of Ben Cichy. There were rumors. Chambliss, who spent a lot of time talking to figures in Seattle's underworld, reported that it was common knowledge Ben Cichy was on the verge of revealing all to investigators when he was killed to shut him up. Drowning, according to Chambliss, was a favorite method of disposing of people in Seattle. Chambliss claimed Cichy's offices at his home were later ransacked, a claim also made by Tony Gustin. But Joel Rindal has dismissed all the innuendo as simply unsubstantiated conspiracy mongering. Yeatts remembers nothing of that day. There were stories that Cichy had a heart condition.

Today, Cichy's death remains what it has been for forty-five years—a mystery. Undeniably, though, many of those who heard about the death at the time assumed Cichy had been murdered. Jessup, for one, testified later that the news immediately left him apprehensive. If there are people alive today who know more about what happened that sunny day on the Yarrow Point dock, they are not saying.

## From Out of the North a Stranger Came, a Law Book in His Hand

Stan Pitkin rightly holds pride of place among those who exposed Seattle's police corruption. Although it took most of 1969 to get him appointed (in the teeth of strenuous opposition by Carroll), in 1970 Pitkin was prepared to make his move. In January of that year, he convened a federal jury to examine gambling and police corruption, the single most important event in the unraveling of the system.

Pitkin had for his use the evidence gathered by Tony Gustin, David Boerner, Reg Bruce, and others working in the attorney general's office, as well as the records from the Lifeline Club raid. He had the strong political backing of Gorton and Evans, and the cooperation of the Palace Guard—Gustin, Corr, and Fuller. Fuller was particularly useful because he had himself participated in payoffs and provided Pitkin with evidence of payoffs he gathered personally from other officers.

*Bryan Johnson of KOMO News pursues US Attorney Stan Pitkin up the courthouse steps.*

But Pitkin faced a hurdle. A US attorney can only investigate and punish violations of federal law. Most of the crimes of which Seattle's police and politicians were suspected of—bribery, graft, gambling, extortion, the odd murder or assault—were state crimes, to be prosecuted, if at all, by the county prosecutor. The single federal law applicable was the one forbidding possession of gambling equipment transported across state lines. This might be enough to go after gamblers with clear interstate ties, like bookmakers. But there was no federal law against local police graft.

Yet Pitkin still succeeded in exposing Seattle's police payoff system because he was aggressive, he was lucky, and a grand jury has some remarkable powers. His luck came in poor Charlie Berger's decision to order improved bingo cards from outside the state, ones on which a player could more easily cover up the numbers called. Previously, Berger had used state-produced cards and given players beans to put on the numbers. By placing that order, Berger violated the one federal law applicable, and Pitkin had the leverage he needed to make an old man confess.

A federal grand jury can subpoena anyone associated with a federal crime and ask them questions about anything reasonably relevant. Starting in January 1970 and continuing over four months in four separate sessions, Pitkin's grand jury called a parade of witnesses, much to the interest of the public and the press, who staked out the entrances and corridors of the courthouse, trying to get pictures of those to be questioned. Because grand juries' proceedings and witness testimony are closely kept secrets, the public only knew the witnesses' names, not their testimony. But in this case, the names were immensely interesting, as they included not just suspected criminals and lowlifes, like Colacurcio and Berger, but also sheriffs and police officers. In fact, the first witness called was Tony Gustin.

Seattle police officers might not have possessed interstate gambling equipment, but they could be asked about those who did. In particular, Pitkin could ask police officers if gamblers or anybody else paid them off. Most denied it, as police officers had done to Dean Leffler's committee, the Blue-Ribbon Committee, and reporters.

But a grand jury is not a citizens' committee. An answer to a grand jury is under oath. Police denials did not end the story. Instead, they set the stage for a possible further federal crime—perjury. In April 1970, after calling him to testify before the grand jury, Pitkin announced that that summer he would be trying former assistant chief Buzz Cook for lying under oath regarding payoffs. Pitkin would call numerous witnesses, many of them cops, to prove two basic points—Seattle police got paid off to ignore criminal activity, and Cook knew it.

Cook's perjury charge was not the only high-profile indictment to come out of Pitkin's grand jury. It also charged Frank Colacurcio, Charles Berger, and their associate Harry Hoffman with the crimes of conspiracy and interstate gambling, and former sheriff Tim McCullough with perjury. The Colacurcio case was eventually moved to Spokane and tried in 1971, and it became its own interesting source of revelations about municipal corruption. Anderson's *Seattle Vice* discusses the trial at some length.

Though Chuck Carroll would not be in either trial, the same thought was on everybody's mind: if the police and sheriff's office were that corrupt, how could Carroll possibly not know?

## CHAPTER 5

# ELECTION

★ ★ ★ ★ ★ ★ ★ ★ ★ ★ ★ ★

### Calculating the Odds

Throughout 1969, my friends and I focused more and more on the idea of one of us running against Chuck Carroll. The political reform movements of the time gave us hope, and the police and Cichy scandals certainly piqued our interest, but ultimately, our real interest in the race was more political.

During the electoral politics of 1968, we and our Republican political allies had had bruising confrontations with the Carroll faction of local Republicans. The faction was rigidly conservative and had been engaged in an ongoing feud with Dan Evans Republicans. The conservatives practiced a type of insular party politics that repelled us. At one point in 1968, in his capacity as county party chair, Ken Rogstad ruled that only those known personally to a precinct committee member were welcome to attend county party caucuses. Infuriated, Evans's allies refused to seat the entire King County delegation at the subsequent state convention.

Carroll was the power behind Rogstad, the colossus astride the system of local party politics. Dan Evans Republicans like my friends and I opposed Rogstad but, unable to unseat him, were interested in removing his main prop by defeating Carroll. The rift in Republican ranks guaranteed any challenge to Carroll could call on an established network of volunteers and allies, veterans of two statewide Evans campaigns. On the other hand, conservative strength in local party battles indicated that challenging Carroll himself would be even more difficult and would face active hostility from the local party organization.

In the wider political world, Carroll's conservative tilt cut both ways. Because these were years when political progressives were becoming more influential in both parties, we could count on at least tacit support from liberals and minority groups in any challenge to Carroll. But for conservatives, Carroll was "tough on crime" and a target of "ultraliberals," both recommendations. The police guild, a political force in its own right, appreciated Carroll's protection of its members.

We had hoped to make Carroll the poster boy for a corrupt system, highlighting his ties to gamblers. But Carroll had stonewalled inquiries regarding the Cichy photograph and the subsequent scandal, and investigations had petered out. *Seattle* magazine, in fact, had suffered financial losses from its decision to go after Carroll, losing the advertising support of some local businesses. And no external criticism of Carroll could discourage his supporters in King County's Republican Party organization.

Political conversations among my friends continued through 1969, though our inner circle's involvement in the actual politics of 1969 was minimal. Lud Kramer, the moderate that AFW helped elect to secretary of state, ran for mayor, and we managed to organize a three-hundred-person rally for him before the September primary. Still, he finished third. First was thirty-four-year-old Democrat state senator Wes Uhlman, and second was a wonderful Establishment figure, Mort Frayn, a respected businessman in his sixties who lost to Uhlman in the final. Everybody liked Frayn, and it was difficult for him to think ill of others, including his friend Chuck Carroll. My favorite memory is the naïveté of his mayoral campaign button, which simply said "MF." Outsiders had to point out that these letters also had another meaning. But though as Republicans we disliked Frayn's loss to Uhlman, we could not but admire Uhlman's victory. He and CHECC veteran Alan Munro put together a modern campaign, with widespread participation and excellent organization. It showed that a race pitched by youth against the Establishment might succeed.

## A Discussion Becomes a Campaign

By the fall of 1969, it was time to begin real planning for a 1970 campaign. The first serious meeting came on September 23, 1969. Those present included the usual crowd—Tom Alberg, George Akers, Bruce Chapman, and Cam Hall—but also new faces like Bill Rodgers (UW law school faculty), Keith Dysart, and Warren Guykema of Gorton's staff. I presided.

Looking back, I am a little startled that this early discussion of a potential opponent to Carroll immediately coalesced around my name. Even among the youthful cadre at the table, my formal qualifications were meager. I had been a lawyer for only three years. My trial experience at Lane Powell consisted of preparing a large courtroom chart illustrating that our client's drug could not have caused the plaintiff's condition. I had been a deputy attorney general for only six months and hadn't gone near a courtroom in that time. It was a "policy" position. Cam Hall and George Akers both had more litigation experience and had been prominent in UW student politics, making them more logical candidates. My dearth of relevant experience left me politically vulnerable, and at the meeting, Alberg noted our number-one priority was to "establish litigation experience so that we have a rebuttal to argument that Bayley has never tried a case."

On the other hand, I had already "gone public," while the others were in the billable hours harnesses of Seattle's top law firms. I had cut my teeth in local politics through CHECC and Action for Washington, and had leadership experience from the Ripon Society and the Harvard Young Republican Club. I enjoyed politics as much as the law and certainly more than the daily law-firm grind. The others simply did not have the time or the interest to risk good jobs on the off chance of beating Carroll and thereby reducing their salaries.

At the September meeting, we started preparing answers to future critics. True, I was only thirty-one, but I wasn't the first one that young to seek the office of prosecuting attorney. Warren Magnuson had been twenty-nine and Scoop Jackson only twenty-six when they became prosecuting attorneys of King and Snohomish Counties, respectively. Carroll himself was only thirty-two on his first run for prosecuting attorney in 1938.

We had a certain cockeyed optimism. Hall mentioned that Tom Foster, who headed the Foster Pepper firm where Hall was an associate, had actually mentioned my name in connection with the race and pledged the magnificent sum of fifty dollars. George Akers opined money would be available, and we discussed getting five to ten "older prestige names" on board early. At the end, someone mentioned we should "leave open the possibility of candidates other than Chris," and the names of Ed Raftis and George Akers were noted in the minutes. But we never discussed these alternatives again. I walked out of the meeting the clear choice, if only by default.

This meeting marked the first time we had chosen to support one of our own, instead of working for others. We were a like-minded group of Republicans, confident, perhaps even arrogant, about our ability to find and fix the problems of Seattle's stale political scene. But we knew all the brilliance we had to command wouldn't be enough to topple a canny, resourceful local politician embedded in the status quo.

Following the September meeting, I circulated a preliminary planning memo on the prosecutor's race. One idea was that Action for Washington could be the campaign vehicle, a chimera that took some time to fade. Bob Davidson, who had risen to Ripon leadership as an undergrad in Cambridge, circulated a long letter making a key political point: "Shady dealings in high places always make good material for 'throw the rascals out' races, but the scanty evidence the *P-I* turned up last summer is certainly not enough to do the trick." I replied at equal length, citing how Wes Uhlman's victory showed that youthful energy in opposition to the Seattle Establishment could be a campaign advantage.

In December, Tom Alberg circulated an assessment and proposal that a new generation of moderate Republican leaders should be following in the wake of Evans, Gorton, and Pritchard by pursuing legislative and congressional races. But Alberg gave those races relatively short shrift before he reached his real point, that the "County Prosecutor's race provides an opportunity to develop tremendous excitement and interest." Alberg warned that Carroll might find it expedient to beg off reelection himself and instead attempt to anoint a successor from inside his office or among his allies, which would result in little real change.

Our early plans got some pushback. Cam Hall was assigned to feel out other attorneys to see if they would support our effort to challenge Carroll. He soon reported back by letter that after thinking about it, he had decided to drop out of our effort. Alberg and I assumed a senior partner had told him I had no chance and he should protect his career. Hall rethought his hesitations later and rejoined us in February.

But we kept going, and after December, the effort moved from the exchange of ideas and names to the practicalities of launching an actual campaign. On January 2, 1970, I convened a lunch to kick the project into a higher gear. This time we included three wise and, hopefully, generous seniors: Fred Baker, John Hauberg, and Shef Phelps. Hauberg and Phelps were the ones who had backed AFW by paying talented young college men $1,000 for the summer to garden and mow their lawns while allowing the "gardeners" to actually cut their political teeth on statewide campaigns. Fred Baker was a seasoned advertising executive and part of the Evans team. At this lunch, we formally resolved that I would enter the prosecutor's race and prepared for the immediate task of convincing people this was realistic. For many, the logic of challenging Carroll made more sense than my doing the challenging. But we convinced ourselves bold thinking was the temper of the times. Charles O. Carroll would get the first serious primary challenge in his career, and I would do the challenging. The only problem was to convince the rest of King County this was a good idea.

## The Campaign

Creating a political campaign is like starting a business designed to close up shop in less than a year. Our principal seed capital was enthusiastic volunteers, but we lacked actual money. The work we did in 1970 would look familiar today: raise money; get endorsements; recruit volunteers; put on events; and arrange doorbelling, mailings, and phone calls. Of course, we also had to churn out numerous releases for the then thriving local press, but we could not have even imagined Twitter.

But elections are as often decided by chance events and external factors as by campaigns. In 1970, we built a strong organization, raised some decent money (eventually), and campaigned hard. But the two most important factors were US Attorney Stan Pitkin's corruption investigation and Washington's blanket primary, which allowed Democrats to cross over and vote for a Republican. Pitkin made police corruption a front-page issue, necessarily trouble for an incumbent prosecutor. And by 1970, the conservative Carroll was a target for Seattle's ascending liberal Democrats, who now controlled the mayor's office and local media outlets. Our most effective messages in the primary turned out to be "Beat Carroll with Bayley" and "Vote September 15." We wanted everybody in Seattle, Democrat or Republican, who was sick of Carroll and what he stood for to vote for me in the primary.

## Spring 1970: Getting the Ball Rolling

My personal go decision was in January, but it took until June 1 to officially kick off the campaign. The intervening months were spent enlisting supporters, raising money, and putting together an actual campaign office—four walls, some phones, campaign materials, and, hopefully, a constant flow of volunteers, mailings, and press releases.

One of our early goals was to break Carroll's lock on local lawyers, whom he pressured every four years for endorsements to be used in large ads in the *Times* and the *P-I*. We preempted him by doing our own survey of King County attorneys, an effort spearheaded by Keith Dysart. We got replies from 377 of the existing 1,750 lawyers. Encouragingly, 317 opposed Carroll's reelection. A resounding 280 would support a "young, serious Republican" against Carroll, though only 101 had heard of me.

At the same time, I conducted my own poll of Seattle's political heavyweights, particularly the Dan Evans faction of Republican moderates. The replies were cautious, but at least most were not opposed. Governor Evans himself was in favor but thought it was a long shot. Gorton, bracingly acerbic as usual, told me to stop being evasive about my plans and campaign openly. Joel Pritchard favored the idea but wanted to know for sure if I was running. He had his own plans that fall, to challenge veteran First District Congressman Tom Pelly in the primary. Our two races would draw upon the same lists of Evans Republicans for volunteers and funds.

My friend Tom Alberg was in charge that spring; he later claimed it was a good thing most of Evans's campaign veterans ended up with Pritchard, because we were free to run a campaign without our mentors looking over our shoulders. Alberg oversaw our meetings and kept track of organizational details. We held some breakfast meetings in the back room of the Dog House on Seventh Avenue, subsequently the Hurricane Café and later swallowed by Amazon development. We looked around one day at the pictures of dogs playing poker on the wall and realized it was probably an illicit card room, of the type we theoretically opposed.

That winter and spring, external events made a reform campaign look ever more plausible. In January, Evans called a special session of the legislature. The session would lead to major state laws on shorelines, clean water, and environmental impact statements, the boon or nemesis of many a major development project for decades to come. Even better, my consumer protection division proposed new legislation strengthening the penalties for fraud. The *Seattle Times* ran an editorial praising the division and me for protecting the consumer. Attached to the article was a photo in which, as usual, I look very young.

Stan Pitkin's grand jury investigation into gambling and payoffs also began in January. Over the next three months, as a succession of law enforcement officials and suspected criminals were hustled into the sealed rooms of the grand jury, the papers ran almost daily stories speculating on their testimony. In February came the indictments of Frank Colacurcio and Charles Berger, and in April the indictment of Buzz Cook for perjury. The Cook trial was of particular interest because it would happen in June, during the campaign. It would be very public and very interesting.

## My Opponents

Carroll's own plans for the election remained a mystery that spring. Ken Rogstad told the press the prosecutor had privately advised him some months before that he planned to retire. But Rogstad said he was trying to change Carroll's mind, given the many leading citizens asking Carroll to reconsider. We assumed that everything Rogstad said was at Carroll's direction and that Carroll was keeping his options open. A few newspapers published stories, citing inside information, that Carroll had secretly decided to run for reelection and was beginning to push his deputies to support him. The man himself, though, maintained a sphinxlike silence.

On the Democratic side, the situation was clearer. Ed Heavey, a King County councilmember and former state representative, announced he would run whether or not the incumbent prosecutor did. The nearly free ride Carroll had had in the last two elections was over.

## Fund—Raising and Fund—Spending

Raising money was never easy. Alberg coordinated the first fund-raising letter, which was sent to other attorneys and netted $2,000. We hoped the key donors to Action for Washington in 1968 would back our cause, but in February, John Hauberg and Shef Phelps told us that after talking it over with their friends at the Rainier Club, they concluded I had no chance and they would not be contributing. This kind of brush off angered more than discouraged me, but fortunately, Alberg was able to change their minds, and they eventually came through.

One of the biggest fish was World's Fair wizard Eddie Carlson, whom *Seattle* magazine had dubbed "Grand Sachem" in its 1968 list of "The Establishment." I wrote Carlson a letter explaining the rationale for my campaign and seeking funds. Carlson's reply was kind but noncommittal. He was "somewhat staggered" by our goal of $50,000, roughly what Mort Frayn had spent running for mayor the year before. (I thought, "Maybe that's why Mort lost.") He then deftly evaded the issue by telling me he was going off on a trip to Asia soon. It would be several more months before I would approach him again.

But by the end of April, we finally had the wherewithal to actually open an office, Room 533 of the Medical Arts Building, a beautiful terra-cotta-clad edifice later demolished to make way for the "Ban Roll-On" building at Second and Seneca. By then I had figured out who would run the campaign. I had discussed the issue with my old friend Richard Allison, then a tutor in Leverett House at Harvard, who surprised me by saying, "Why don't I do it?" I had not known his army service in Vietnam had included organizing a global parcel service, mostly freight, for both the Department of Defense and the NSA. Richard would arrive in June and live with Bruce Chapman and me in our Magnolia bachelor pad. Bob Davidson, a precocious Harvard junior, signed up as deputy campaign manager. It turned out to be a great team.

## Not Quite a Candidate

I maintained a public profile as deputy attorney general, moderating a series of panels on crime on KCTS 9, a public TV station, as part of its Law in Action series. Gorton appeared with me once on a show about the Washington State Legislature, and afterward, I ensured that would never happen again. As I explained to Dave Boerner, who also worked in the attorney general's office:

> I plan to ask Slade *not* to be on the "crime" programs, as he naturally assumes the center of attention when he is on and I am the moderator. In fact, the one on the legislative session last night pointed this out well. . . . I know diddly about the legislature compared to the boss, and because he has a whole string of questions ready so I ended up just starting and ending the program.

By April, I had been unofficially running for office for three months while officially still on the public payroll. The incongruity was starting to show. That month, Neale Chaney of the Washington State Democrats wrote to Alberg telling him I was a candidate and should resign from the attorney general's office. Chaney also wrote to KVI, a radio station, telling them to kick me off as host of *Con Man Out*. Alberg responded to both Chaney and KVI that I had not declared my candidacy, and therefore there were no restrictions on my actions. He added that Ed Heavey was also making candidate-like noises and probably should resign from the King County Council.

But in truth, I was mixing public and political activities in a way that would not pass scrutiny today. We didn't keep track of office time used for the campaign, and my return address on political memos and letters was 1266 Dexter Horton Building, the Seattle office of the attorney general! Chastened by Chaney's intervention, I instructed my deputy Bill Clarke to ensure any political efforts made inside my office were on personal time.

## The Outside World

I was focused on the campaign, but in Seattle and all over the country that spring was when Vietnam War protests and urban violence reached a crescendo.

On February 17, protesters marched on the Federal Courthouse downtown, angry at the Chicago Seven trial then going on. Up to five thousand people ended up massed on Fifth Avenue between the courthouse and the library. A few broke windows and caused other minor but expensive destruction.

In May, violence returned. On May 1, President Nixon ordered the invasion of Cambodia, to deprive the North Vietnamese of safe havens. Four days later, Ohio National Guard troops fired on antiwar demonstrators at Kent State University, killing four students and wounding others. On May 5, reacting to Cambodia and Kent State, thousands of protesters at the University of Washington marched down Forty-Fifth Street and then onto I-5, shutting down the freeway. That protest was peaceful, but later protests on the UW campus itself were met with a brutal police response.

And finally, on May 15, Seattle police shot and killed Larry Ward immediately after he placed a homemade bomb at Hardcastle Realty at Twenty-Fourth and Union in the Central District. Rumors began flying that the police had set up the bombing and that Ward was a dupe. The black community immediately called for an investigation of this killing of a black man by a white officer under suspicious circumstances. Carroll's refusal to prosecute any of the police officers involved further poisoned his name in the black community.

## The Lion in His Den

My most memorable event that May was a courtesy call on the prosecuting attorney, arranged by his old friend and my mentor, Mort Frayn. I wish I could capture the raspy Frayn voice, a friendly version of Brando in *The Godfather*, saying, "You really should call on Chuck and tell him your plans."

Frayn and I arrived at the courthouse, went up to Carroll's fifth-floor office, and found him at the head of his huge mahogany conference table, flanked by his closest political companions, Bill Boeing Jr. and Victor Denny. Besides having been Carroll's campaign chair in 1962 and 1966, Denny was a direct descendant of one of Seattle's founders. Boeing, sometimes described as a walking political checkbook, chaired the finance committee for the local Republican Party and carried his own famous name. It was a triptych of power, designed to scare the hell out of me.

I politely informed the three I intended to run for King County prosecutor. Carroll was not pleased and launched into a speech explaining how unthinkable this was. He told me about the red telephone by his bed, which would ring in the dark of night, summoning him to the scene of a crime. (After succeeding him, I learned he was at least properly equipped for nighttime runs. His 1969 Bonneville county car had red lights and a siren hidden in the grill.) Carroll pointed out he had several senior deputies who had tried many murder cases, and none of *them* were qualified to succeed him. I did not try to contradict him with my record of two district court appearances.

His tirade over, there was little for me to say, so Frayn and I provided pleasant good-byes and left the trio. They were probably unworried about this upstart who dared to challenge them. Personally, I felt pleasantly liberated from some of my previous fear of the man. One on one, Carroll was a self-satisfied blowhard.

Back at the office, the pieces fell into place. I wrote Gorton a letter requesting a leave of absence, which he granted effective June 1. Always practical, he added that if everything did not pan out, I could come back, either in September or November. Our formal kickoff on May 30 went well, with lots of press, including the eager *P-I* and *Seattle* magazine.

By then, Ed Heavey was in the open too. Soon after our kickoff, Citizens for Heavey sent the press a broadside accusing Carroll's office of soliciting lawyer support for the boss in violation of American Bar Association canons. In the race that followed, Heavey and I would be running on parallel paths.

## Coffee and Anonymity

I was under the radar through most of June. My focus was introductions to the editors of regional papers, enlisting law students to draft white papers on the wonderful reforms we would accomplish after winning, and arranging for coffee hours in local homes. The latter were great preparation for debates and TV; I learned to look people in the eye and to know the issues inside out so my face didn't betray uncertainty. My staffers were merciless afterward, pointing out when I looked over my audience's head or gave complex answers that didn't respond to the question. Coffee-hour logistics are precise. The campaign provided hosts with a memo laying out the timing of my arrival (twenty minutes after the coffee hour begins) and departure (after about a half hour of banter). Only then would the host pitch for money. These logistics were developed after a catastrophe at one early coffee hour when my driver didn't come back on time and I was trapped making conversation for over an hour.

But coffee hours, newspaper interviews, and issue papers wouldn't topple Carroll. In June, one could tell, just by the tone of conversations, that people saw my cause as noble but doomed. Contributions stayed nominal. One attorney at a downtown law office had publicly promised $1,000 to anyone who would oppose Carroll. When we attempted to collect, he was suddenly unavailable. Carroll looked unbeatable, and everybody knew he held grudges against those who opposed him. Some of our money came from people who contributed only because they thought Carroll wouldn't run.

## Providence Provides Pitkin

Near the end of June, fortune smiled. The federal grand jury investigations had piqued people's interest, but the scandal of police payoffs did not really have an impact until Buzz Cook's perjury trial began on June 23. Each day for the next two weeks, trial testimony was repeated on the front pages of both the *Times* and the *P-I*, plus follow-up features on the inside pages. US attorney Stan Pitkin called numerous witnesses, including police officers, each testifying the payoff system was so widespread that Cook must have known about it.

More than any other event, before or after, the Cook trial broke open the conspiracy of silence surrounding the payoff system. The trial showed graft in Seattle was not a matter of one or two policemen occasionally accepting a free cup of coffee, a bottle of liquor, a few dollars. The graft was widespread, long term, substantial, and systematic. It went as high up in the police department as the available witnesses could testify to. The problem was no longer ignorable and the status quo was unacceptable.

None of the witnesses directly implicated Carroll. But journalists looked for spin-off stories to augment their trial coverage. We hastily wrote a press release for the campaign—"Bayley demands

Carroll act!" and then got the *P-I* to run it, almost verbatim, as a news story. Unlike Ross Cunningham and the *Seattle Times*, the editor of the *P-I*, Lou Guzzo, hated Carroll. Guzzo had pushed for the Cichy photographs in 1968, and his opinion of Carroll had not changed. The *P-I* was always happy to receive our press releases and published many. To connect Carroll with the police scandal, we emphasized his passivity in the presence of corruption. We noted he took no interest in police payoffs, even after all the scandals and stories that had begun in 1967 and continued through Tony Gustin's Lifeline Club raid. We pointed out the Tolerance Policy was the root of the problem and Carroll refused to challenge the policy. I cited Gorton's letter to Carroll in the summer of 1969 that suggested he look into evidence of graft; Carroll never followed up. We did not mention the Cichy photograph. Reporters were more than willing to bring that up themselves.

On July 9, the jury found Buzz Cook guilty of perjury, and we issued more press releases calling on Carroll to act on the trial evidence.

Meanwhile, the campaign really began humming. We had a campaign newsletter and a band of enthusiastic volunteers ready to doorbell and pass out leaflets. Among them were young women dubbed the "Bayley Girls," who were new to campaigning but were a significant asset. Among this group shone Shelley Pemberton, Christine Yorozu, my cousin Vinny Dunn, Patsy Andrews, and many others, whose enthusiasm for campaigning was contagious. When I was shaking hands with business owners or listening carefully to some senior citizen, I usually had next to me a fresh faced, smiling young woman wearing a Bayley button.

As for Carroll himself, that July he departed for an extended cruise to northern waters on his elegant 1930s yacht *Shearwater* without tipping his hand as to his intentions. We thought running against Carroll in the primary would be the toughest test, but in retrospect, we were wrong: the anti-Carroll crusade was the only real dynamic throughout the campaign.

## August—Money and Drama

Carroll filed on the last day possible, the Friday of the first week of August. He told the press he wanted to continue serving the public and it was important to save the office from his unqualified opponents. Carroll had always been proud of his office and his accumulated political power. But he also had something to lose if he did not run. After the Cook trial, a grand jury was inevitable, and he probably wanted to control it.

Later that Friday, after hearing Carroll filed, Lem Howell also filed in the Democratic primary. This initially worried us. A competitive race on the Democratic side could attract the Democrats we needed for the primary. But as it turned out, Howell was a blessing. He ran because he was angry; he had represented Larry Ward's family at the inquest. That August, Howell went after Carroll, flat out accusing him of being crooked, language I would never have attempted, which generated its own headlines.

Our biggest concern that August was money. We had the *P-I* and enthusiasm and legions of volunteers leading me through Seafair events, but none of those pay for advertising. We needed to raise $30,000 for mailings, radio ads, and maybe even TV commercials before the September 15 primary. And now that Carroll had filed, some of our previous financial supporters were asking for their money back. I wrote letters to everyone I could think of, seeking large dollar donations. It didn't help that Joel Pritchard's primary campaign was fishing in the same pools. And this was also the year Boeing went bust, laying off thirty-five thousand of its eighty thousand workers in the course of the year.

*Lem Howell, a lively democratic primary candidate, helps me by attacking Chuck Carroll.*

A $1,000 contribution from my mother's old friend Eleanor Frazier was one of the few bright spots. Mrs. Frazier was an exception to the rule that wealthy widows hang on to their cash. More typical was my call on my brother Jon's godmother, Katherine Baillargeon, part of one of Seattle's famous old families. We had a pleasant visit in her dark house on Capitol Hill, where she served tea and made wonderful noises about "of course" contributing to the campaign. I made the rookie error of not pulling out a remit envelope and asking her right then and there for a significant sum like a hundred dollars. Instead, I left the envelope, and a few days later we opened it at headquarters and extracted her ten-dollar check.

Early in August, we had a nasty surprise when John Strachan, our media consultant, demanded immediate payment on a $10,000 bill that we had set aside for later, waiting for the campaign to prosper. This created a fund-raising emergency, postponed for a bit by

Richard Allison and George Akers going to Strachan's office to bully him into providing more specific billing, but ultimately solved only by help from the reliable John Hauberg and Shef Phelps and the rising tide of contributions.

The money woes were offset by political winds blowing our way. The press diligently covered several preprimary debates, all of them anti-Carroll events. The prosecutor never appeared (once, he said, because it was his birthday), but at the end of the month, we pulled off one of the great coups in Seattle political history by tracking him down.

## Lake City Ambush

Through most of August, we had not been able to smoke out Carroll for a public confrontation. So we put Keith Dysart on the case, and I checked in with him from phone booths several times a day for Carroll's latest movements. I was at Garfield High School early in the evening of August 24 when Keith reported Carroll was headed for a meeting with the reliably conservative Forty-Sixth District Republican Club in Lake City. Keith then alerted the *P-I* and KING TV, while my teenage driver raced me to the Lake City library. There we saw Carroll's deputy Neal Shulman on the outside pay phone. Shulman had spotted the press and was trying to warn Carroll off but failed. Carroll arrived anyway, and we took seats in the back.

Just as Carroll was introduced, Dysart stood up and asked why he refused to debate his opponent. Carroll shot back that he would meet me anywhere, at which point I stood up and marched to the front.

The chair announced there would be no actual debate, but that did not stop us from attacking each other. Though taken by surprise,

*We forced Carroll out into the open in an impromptu debate at the Lake City Library.*

Carroll kept his balance. He denounced Rockefeller Republicans and claimed the Ripon Society was raising $50,000 for my election. I responded concisely that Carroll was lying. (I would have loved to receive $50,000 from Ripon, but that wasn't happening. My friends in Ripon were attempting nationwide fund-raising for a number of candidates that year. They managed a total of $5,000, of which I received $3,000 late in the campaign. Other recipients included George H. W. Bush in Texas and John Ashcroft in Missouri.) He then brought up my courtesy call on him in May, saying he had been undecided about running again "and hoped to find a qualified candidate," but that after meeting me and learning I had never tried a case, decided to stay. I noted I had more experience than Carroll had when he first ran in 1938. Dysart piped up from the back, asking when Carroll had last tried a case. Carroll admitted it had been many years but he'd been very busy.

The audience belonged to Carroll; they applauded him heartily and interrupted me occasionally. "We came to hear Carroll," one shouted. But the press ran my way. The next morning, the *P-I* had a photo of me confronting Carroll, and KING TV had two minutes of shadowy footage. Even the *Times* ran a story. It was predictably proincumbent ("Carroll was bold, full of fight, and looked like a veteran political pro—which he was—enjoying a campaign encounter"), but it did point out that afterward, the prosecutor refused to meet me again before the primary.

The ambush and the resulting press were shots in the arm. Volunteers and donations increased, and there was a palpable change in the atmosphere. People who had been politely interested in June were seriously committed by late August. Richard Allison remembers walking down a street at the end of August, seeing a TV in a storefront window showing a story about the race, turning to me, and saying, "You know, we might actually win this."

## Sunny Days

As August turned into September, Bayley signs began blossoming on lawns across the city. Signs are more an indicator of volunteer enthusiasm than they are a predictor of elections, but still, they were a great morale boost.

I was out on a tight schedule of debates, fund-raisers, walking tours of neighborhoods, and newspaper interviews, but the real work came in the doorbelling, mailings, and making phone calls. Early computer geek Steve Murphy capitalized on after-hours access to UW mainframes to mathematically pinpoint key precincts. Coincidentally, some teenagers from Lakeside School were roaming UW's computer labs those evenings. Paul Allen's father was a campus librarian, and with the key they borrowed, Allen and his schoolmate Bill Gates spent that same summer learning how to use computers.

By primary day, we had contacted 250,000 voters who might be supporters, using data from Evans's and Gorton's elections, reasonable proxies for my own campaign. The Carroll-controlled King County Republicans refused to provide their database, but State Chair Gummie Johnson helped us acquire state voter records.

Many of the smaller papers were on our side. I particularly enjoyed the *Mercer Island Reporter*, which said my schedule read like a timetable for a shuttle service and my "press releases hit editors' desks with the regularity of an expertly-swung sledgehammer."

The reformers in the police department became interested. Eugene Corr, a member of the Palace Guard, took to visiting the campaign office in the evening and distracting workers with tales of Carroll's malign influence on the police department, stories unfortunately light on useful details.

Carroll's campaign, by contrast, was nearly invisible. His office consisted of a storefront with an unlisted number, actually more of a materials warehouse. Carroll was supported by King County's Republican district organizations, but as far as we could tell, very few people actually knocked on doors. Carroll's "volunteers" were in large part his own staff and not always very enthusiastic. One of these was a secretary named Cathy Wright. She agreed to address envelopes for Carroll at night but then thought better of it, on the advice of her husband, a police officer opposed to Carroll. When she told Carroll the next day, she admitted she might not vote for him either. "You don't know who you are going to vote for? Well, maybe you better not work here anymore," Carroll replied. Soon after, he fired her.

Carroll chiefly relied on newspaper ads and a campaign brochure with sixteen arguments recycled from previous campaigns (for example, that Carroll founded the King County Salacious

Literature Committee, which he created in the 1950s and by 1970 was mostly a relic). Carroll made a few safe campaign appearances like the one we invaded in Lake City but otherwise used surrogates, such as prominent conservative attorney Stuart Oles, who attacked Carroll's critics in a speech before the Young Men's Republican Club. Oles was not particularly convincing, claiming Ben Cichy was a respectable businessman.

Carroll mostly kept his distance from the papers, speaking only to the *Times* and some suburban papers. He boycotted the *P-I* entirely, calling it his fourth challenger, after Howell, Heavey, and me. Carroll's reluctance to appear publicly was similar to his previous campaigns. Before, though, he'd been in a position of strength. Now, even friendly reporters asked about his association with Ben Cichy, a detail he refused to explain right up to the end. For some, the silence itself was a sticking point. The editor of the Auburn *Globe News*, John Fournier, wrote that unless Carroll explained his association with Cichy, Fournier would endorse me.

## Carroll Votes in "Hoax" Poll

Anticipating Carroll's attorney endorsement ads, we sought the help of the Young Lawyers of the King County Bar Association to organize a bar poll in August. Democrat Llew Pritchard was a strong supporter, and the group as a whole disliked Carroll, particularly his practice of strong-arming the county's lawyers into supporting him every four years.

The Young Lawyers mailed a "ballot" with a choice of Howell, Heavey, Bayley, or Carroll to all 1,750 members of the King County Bar Association. The completed ballot went into an anonymous security envelope, which was then mailed in an outer envelope signed by the participant, like today's vote-by-mail process. The poll received a healthy 1,144 responses, and I was on top, with just under half of all votes (Bayley 567, Carroll 385, Heavey 125, Howell 67). Carroll declared the poll a hoax, cueing Dave Hoff, who chaired the Young Lawyers, to summon the press and hold up an outer enve- lope with Carroll's customary green ink signature, proving he had participated in the hoax and his vote had been counted. The bar poll became part of our final advertisements. Carroll's best weapon was turned against him.

Another of Carroll's props, his police allies, also failed him. The leadership of the Seattle Police Officers' Guild endorsed him, but the endorsement caused younger officers to revolt. In two days, they collected 303 signatures (approximately 25 percent of the member- ship) on a petition to rescind the endorsement. That story hit the papers at the same time as the scuffle over the bar poll.

On the other hand, we still had no friend in the *Seattle Times*. Ross Cunningham referred darkly to the contest against Carroll as a "lynching party" ginned up by "ultraliberals." And Carroll also maintained the backing of a significant share of organized labor.

## Penultimate Victory

Our radio ads intoned, "Vote September 15," and in the days leading up to the primary, we supplemented the advertising blitz by hand- ing out leaflets to passersby. Tom Alberg, Cam Hall, Norm Maleng, and other volunteers joined me in staking out Seattle's downtown street corners on September 14. Given the excitement and momen- tum, we thought we had a real chance, perhaps 50–50, to defeat the undefeatable Carroll.

The election party itself was at the Olympic Hotel, where I arrived shortly after the first returns. By then, the good news had swept through the crowd. All the returns were good. We were triumphant;

we had slain the dragon. It was clear it wasn't even going to be close. I beat Carroll by forty thousand votes. We were giddy that night. I kept finding the eyes of my friends on me as we couldn't stop grinning. A year before, we had been just a few people huddled around a table trying to convince ourselves we had a chance. And now we were here, surrounded by a happy, triumphant crowd.

I got a letter the next day from Elizabeth Anderson, who had once worked for Carroll (which she described as "six miserable years as Chief Civil Clerk for 'God'"): "For the first time since I worked for him and left his office in 1967 I can breathe freely, and the horrible anxiety that has been with me for so long has left with your victory."

*A proud Dorothy Bayley accompanies her ecstatic son into a primary night victory party.*

## Staggering to the Finish

My primary victory was almost too complete. The huge crossover vote from Democrats gave me almost as many votes as all the other candidates combined, and the large margin made us complacent. The loss of energy was palpable, even more so as we lost student volunteers to the start of school and Assistant Manager Bob Davidson headed back to Harvard.

Plus, Ed Heavey was a more difficult opponent than Carroll. With Carroll gone, Democrats returned to their fold, and Heavey was quickly endorsed by Martin Durkan, Wes Uhlman, and other prominent Democrats. Fortunately, Senator Scoop Jackson stayed out of the race, influenced by our ally Phil Bailey, publisher of the *Argus*, who hosted an election night dinner at the Sunset Club for both Jackson and me.

We still lacked cash. In the primary, we spent $51,000 but only raised $42,000. We'd thrown it all into the primary, and even that was barely enough. Advertisements in the Sunday *Times* prior to the primary election had been financed in part by the personal checks of Cam Hall and Keith Dysart. We had nothing left for ongoing expenses or further advertising. When Heavey suggested a limit of $25,000 for final election spending, we quickly accepted. Our campaigns never agreed how to enforce a limit, but everybody assumed $25,000 was the upper number.

But even $25,000 was a push to find. Again, Bailey helped out. Richard Allison and I laid our cards on the table at his offices in the old White-Henry-Stuart building. Bailey had already promised free advertising, but I confessed our needs went deeper. Bailey's response was immediate—"Let's call Eddie." He then picked up his phone, dialed, and said, "Eddie, this is Phil. We need your help."

Eddie, of course, was Edward E. Carlson, Seattle's inimitable impresario, whom I had approached unsuccessfully in the spring.

He'd been skeptical before, but now, in the glow of my primary victory, he jumped in. Carlson knew everybody with influence in Seattle, and he could get most of them to come to his famous working breakfasts, held at seven o'clock at the Golden Lion, downstairs at the Olympic Hotel. He formed a group called 100 for 100—that is, ten people who committed to contacting ten other people, all of whom would contribute $100 each. And true to his word, he was able to raise about $10,000.

Though short of funds, we still had enough volunteers and donations to continue a visible campaign. The Teamsters, under the leadership of Arnie Weinmeister, switched from Carroll to us after the primary—Lord knows why. The Teamsters provided a magnificent bus, which was previously used for Senator Magnuson's elections and was equipped with a speaker's platform on the back, an icebox, a coffee machine, and a driver and bullhorn operator. Richard Allison joked that at last I had my version of Air Force One.

In the final election, I needed to sell myself again and define a new opponent. Before most audiences, I was a young reformer, running against a member of the Old Courthouse Gang. For partisan Republicans, I was also a longstanding Republican who would keep an important office in safe hands. I met with the King County Republican Central Committee, Carroll's true believers, and explained my problems were with Carroll's policies, not Carroll. The reception was frosty. I managed a joint appearance with Congressman Tom Pelly, who had just fended off Joel Pritchard, but then had to find excuses to avoid having my picture taken with Carroll.

Unlike Carroll, Heavey enjoyed campaigning, and could be eloquent and funny at the podium. Perhaps our most important debate was at Lincoln High School, my alma mater. There, *P-I* reporter Shelby Scates asked us how we would vote on Referendum 20, an abortion rights measure on the November ballot.

Heavey bobbed and weaved: he had not made up his mind, though he didn't believe in abortions, but the present law discriminated against the poor, although their interests must be balanced against community mores. He ended with "It's up to each individual to make up his mind."

My own answer was more direct: as a Roman Catholic, I personally opposed abortion but felt neither I nor the state had the right to make a woman's decision for her. I would vote for Referendum 20. The abortion rights people were unhappy I opposed abortion, but abortion opponents were livid I would vote for the referendum. I received several angry letters castigating me for my "cowardice," and on subsequent Sundays, windshields in Catholic church parking lots were covered with leaflets denouncing me. My unprepared answer on this controversial issue was probably a factor in the election. My guess is it cost me votes, though at least a few Democrats told me Heavey's equivocation tilted them against him.

## Heavey versus Bayley

Issues counted less in the final than backgrounds. Heavey and I both ran reform campaigns. But Heavey had been in the state legislature and was on the King County Council, while I had zero elective experience. And Heavey was a Democrat, like the majority of voters in King County.

Our actual policy conflicts focused most sharply on the looming grand jury. Heavey wanted it to be conducted by an independent prosecutor selected by judges, while I promised to lead the investigation myself. The seemingly small difference in procedure stemmed from a larger difference in philosophy. Heavey saw the prosecutor's office as inherently partisan and necessarily predisposed in everything to act politically, most particularly grand juries. In one debate he got very worked up on this point. His voice rising, Heavey told the audience there was no possibility of either of us leading a neutral investigation, citing the experience under Carroll:

> We all know that grand juries are the most political thing in King County since they were invented. The name of the game in 1966 was get Wallace. Well, they got Scott Wallace. . . . Grand juries under a partisan, elected politician are politics, that's all they are.

I disagreed. I said then, and still think now, that the prosecuting attorney can be above partisanship and should make all decisions, including those involving grand juries, in a nonpartisan way. I intended to use the grand jury to investigate the Tolerance Policy and the police payoff system in a manner that favored no person or party.

## By a Nose

In the last couple of weeks, we were still optimistic; we had no money for polling to tell us otherwise. We raised $20,000 but, as of the buy deadline on October 28, were short the additional $5,000 needed for radio or TV ads. We doubled down on bus signs and newspaper ads for the final week and crossed our fingers. And then came the puppet ads.

They appeared in the daily papers in the week before the election: tall, skinny cartoons stretching up half an entire page, showing a caricature of Dan Evans holding the strings to an owl-eyeglassed Slade Gorton, who was in turn manipulating the small figure of yours truly in a Little Lord Fauntleroy suit. The ads struck at my youth and lack of experience, and implied reformers Evans and

Gorton were a sinister force out to control King County. Political insiders chuckled at the thought of Dan Evans manipulating Slade Gorton. But the ads probably had an impact on the broad public.

The cartoon was signed by "H. N. Tibbetts" of the "Committee for Responsible Law Enforcement," both names unknown. It turned out Tibbetts was a stooge acting on behalf of Ken Monson, editor of the Boeing machinists newspaper called the *Aero Mechanic*, who raised the $8,000 needed to fund the ad from undisclosed sources. The financing was never resolved, before or after the election. Heavey adamantly denied knowing anything about it. Monson was proud of his ability to design the ad but never revealed his backing. Ken Rogstad admitted visiting another Democrat, Ken Sanwick, who was also doing some work for Heavey. But Rogstad denied providing help to Heavey's campaign, directly or indirectly.

All we could do was dismiss the ads and hope for the best. Evans and Gorton issued a press release attempting to simultaneously praise my character and deny their influence. They also sent me a gift, which I opened up the night of the election in front of the press—a bright red puppet. We were fortunate the campaign ended when it did. Another week of those ads, and I'm sure I would have lost.

Election night, November 3, was not as much fun as the primary. I rented a room upstairs from our Olympic Hotel victory party and had the misfortune to be right next to Scoop Jackson's inner circle gathering. Their revels lasted until dawn, and I didn't get much sleep. By the end of a tense evening, I was in fact behind, though not by much. But there were lots of mail-in votes outstanding, and Republicans had long held an edge among absentees.

All Heavey and I could do was wait while our representatives monitored the vote count. The results came in slowly, but the trend lines were always good. Dysart provided the "Bayley Prayer Club" with elaborate mathematical calculations showing my election was

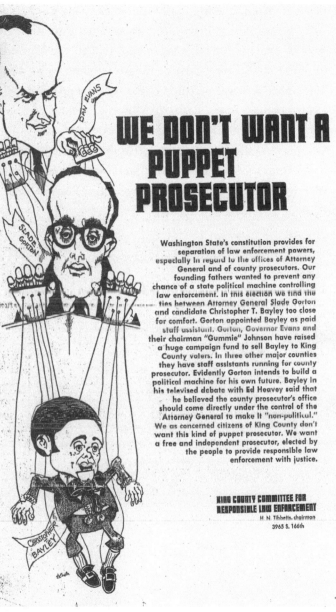

# WE DON'T WANT A PUPPET PROSECUTOR

Washington State's constitution provides for separation of law enforcement powers, especially in regard to the offices of Attorney General and of county prosecutors. Our founding fathers wanted to prevent any chance of a state political machine controlling law enforcement. In this election we find the ties between Attorney General Slade Gorton and candidate Christopher T. Bayley too close for comfort. Gorton appointed Bayley as paid staff assistant. Gorton, Governor Evans and their chairman "Gummie" Johnson have raised a huge campaign fund to sell Bayley to King County voters. In three other major counties they have staff assistants running for county prosecutor. Evidently Gorton intends to build a political machine for his own future. Bayley in his televised debate with Ed Heavey said that he believed the county prosecutor's office should come directly under the control of the Attorney General to make it "non-political." We as concerned citizens of King County don't want this kind of puppet prosecutor. We want a free and independent prosecutor, elected by the people to provide responsible law enforcement with justice.

**KING COUNTY COMMITTEE FOR RESPONSIBLE LAW ENFORCEMENT**
H. N. Tibbetts, chairman
3965 S. 166th

*In a last minute ad, my opponent portrays me as a hapless puppet to Governor Dan Evans and Attorney General Slade Gorton.*

all but guaranteed. The final tally was so close—a gap of less than half of 1 percent—that it required an automatic recount. During the wait, I made plans for a recruiting trip to the University of Washington law school—new staffing was going to be a priority. On December 2, it was certified that I was the new King County prosecutor by 1,453 votes. Richard Allison gave me a silver martini pitcher with the number engraved on the side.

And thus, finally, I had the opportunity I demanded, to reform the prosecutor's office. But while tackling that job, there was another task requiring immediate attention. Seattle finally, formally needed to investigate its own.

# CHAPTER 6

# TRIAL

★ ★ ★ ★ ★ ★ ★ ★ ★ ★ ★ ★

I was prosecutor for two terms—eight years—during which I tackled a number of problems. But by promise and public clamor, my priority for the first term was to clean up the past—a county grand jury and subsequent indictments and trials targeting municipal corruption. I began the investigation on my arrival in January 1971, and litigation continued through criminal convictions and guilty pleas in late 1973 and early 1974. It was the last act in the drama that started with the Wilson Twins' story in 1967, the final reckoning in a betrayal of the public trust that went back many years.

By the time I arrived, there had already been significant changes to Seattle's political system. Police no longer took payoffs. There was a new police chief, George Tielsch, who did not tolerate graft of any sort. The city had a new mayor to accompany a rapidly evolving city council, and King County had its first executive. All this plus Carroll's removal as prosecutor knocked most of the existing props out from under the system. Some felt nothing more needed doing.

They were wrong. In 1971, the senior leadership of a police department that had reaped sizable sums from payoffs was still largely intact. The rank and file knew payoffs had once been common and money had been made. Until the culture of self-profit itself ended, systematic police graft could return. An incorruptible new police chief could help, but chiefs come and go, while bureaucracies remain. The police "gold braid" could wait Tielsch out, and they had their own voice in city hall in the person of Wayne Larkin, former head of the Seattle Police Officers' Guild, who remained a city councilmember until 1978.

Nor had Stan Pitkin's work eliminated Seattle's market for commercial vice. Profits from illegal and legal gambling would continue to be available to help out potential friends. There would be new elections and new legislative proposals to adjust the boundaries of allowable vice, and new opportunities for campaign contributions to influence the results.

King County needed to clean up its own act and do so publicly and relentlessly, to permanently discourage those coming later. Besides, indicting likely criminals was the right thing to do. If I ignored the past crimes, I would be sending a new message—that the law does not touch the well connected. I wince, still, when I think of the problems and errors that dogged the county's corruption investigation and trials. But I have no regrets about what we attempted.

## Pitkin's Trial—Buzz Cook a Liar?

The federal trial in summer 1970 made possible all we did at the county level. I've described its impact on my campaign in June. But the trial itself deserves a little more attention.

The federal indictment charged M. E. "Buzz" Cook, an assistant police chief, with perjury. In years past, prior to the IACP-inspired reorganization, Cook had been second only to the chief and had also been directly in charge of the patrol division, which constituted 80 to 85 percent of the police force. He was the only assistant chief in 1969 not to join the Palace Revolt. After Chief Frank Ramon's departure, Cook was the highest-ranking officer Pitkin could have targeted.

Before the federal grand jury in early 1970, Cook was asked, among other things, three broad questions to which he gave three flat denials:

**Q.** Do you have any knowledge of law enforcement officers being paid by operators of gambling establishments? **A.** *No, I do not.*

**Q.** You don't have any knowledge of anybody currently on the force who participated in shakedowns? **A.** *I do not.*

**Q.** Have you at any time received any money, property, or thing of value from any person, direct or indirect, who has been involved in gambling activities? **A.** *No.*

Pitkin alleged these three answers, under oath, were lies.

Witnesses in the Cook trial were bar owners and police officers, those who paid and those who took the payments. Much of the testimony was essentially accounting. For example, MacIver Wells, whose complaints were what initially interested the Wilson Twins in the police payoffs, explained how he began by paying $35 per month for one tavern and eventually ended up paying $270 per month for three locations. Police officers testified the system included payoffs for each beat, plus separate payoffs to the vice squad. The rule was the patrol officers kept half and then passed half up the line. Similarly, captains would keep half and pass half up to their assistant chief. Because the patrol officers and vice squad were paid the same amounts, separately, each could check with the other to make sure neither was being shortchanged.

The testimony also revealed the system's history, its extent, and its occasional disruptions. Some highlights:

- Wesley Moore, formerly a Seattle police officer, took payoffs as early as 1936—twenty-dollar bribes occasionally paid by bail bondsmen. Others testified to payoffs made in the forties, fifties, and sixties.

- Previous investigations disrupted the payoff system but never ended it. A bar owner testified that in 1958, payoffs were suspended while the new mayor, Gordon Clinton, was investigating the police. But the pause only lasted a couple of months. The police suspended payoffs again in 1966 and early 1967, the result of the FBI report by MacIver Wells, the Wilson Twins articles, and the work of the Blue-Ribbon Committee. But all these pauses were only temporary, until the last suspension at the end of August 1968.

- Payoffs implicated the highest-ranking police officers. Payoffs were made to Chief H. J. Lawrence from 1952 to 1961, as well as to former assistant chief Charles Rouse. People also testified to directing payoffs to Cook. There was no direct testimony implicating former chief Ramon, but some testified to collecting money for him. It was claimed the current acting chief, Frank Moore, then being groomed by Uhlman to be the chief, had helped pass the word in 1968 to shut down the payoff system and await further orders.

- The payoff system and its protectors extended beyond the police department. Witnesses reported thirdhand allegations that Charles M. Carroll, chair of the city council's licensing committee, received $300 per month from the vice squad. Several testified they brought complaints regarding the payoff system to either Mayor Braman or his aides and got little help.

- Prosecutor Carroll figured only by his absence. When an officer who wanted to protest the payoffs was asked whether he thought it would have helped to go to Carroll, he answered, simply, no.

On July 9, the jury found Cook guilty, beginning a long series of appeals. (Several years later, a court would reverse Cook's perjury conviction, finding that Cook could reasonably have understood questions about payoffs to relate to the date on which he was asked, February 1970, instead of a previous date.) Attention turned to the rest of Seattle's police department.

## Mistakes Were Made, but Let's Move On

Between the end of the Cook trial in July 1970 and January 1971, events took three tracks.

Stan Pitkin brought more charges, most notably trying former sheriff McCullough in November on the same charge he'd used against Cook—perjury. The trial of Frank Colacurcio and Charles Berger, in Spokane, also consumed Pitkin's time. But none of this broke new ground or caused the same impact as the Cook trial.

In the Seattle Police Department, there was some rapid turnover at the top. Acting Chief Frank Moore was tarnished by the Cook trial testimony and pleaded the Fifth Amendment when called before Pitkin's grand jury. Mayor Uhlman replaced him with two short-term acting chiefs, first Charles Gain and then Edward Toothman, both on leave from regular jobs in California. Gain was Oakland's police chief, so he was experienced with troubled police forces.

Gain, who was in office for a month, appointed Toothman to head a police department task force to investigate graft. When Gain returned to California, Toothman took over for another month.

Toothman's task force interviewed hundreds of police officers, including many who had not testified before the federal grand jury. Unfortunately, the task force was resisted by the Seattle Police Officers' Guild, which went to court to stop polygraph examinations of police officers. The court enjoined the polygraphs, slowing down the investigation and encouraging officers who were stonewalling.

Ultimately, the task force collected enough information to uncover most of the payoff system. On September 14, it published a report, along with a confidential annex with details of particular police misbehavior. The public report acknowledged the payoff system had endured for years and involved systematic extortion of businesses. But it also minimized the rot and deflected blame.

> The question is asked, "How extensive was the involvement in terms of numbers of officers?" It has been stated earlier that only a few districts were involved. At a given period, there were about 35 to 40 men working in these districts. Of that number, all were not involved. There is only speculation as to how many were. Of those who worked in the department during the last ten years, the Task Force identified about 70 to 80 as having been involved in payoffs. The majority of those persons had left the Police Department prior to the beginning of the investigation....
>
> It must be remembered, however, that there were many persons other than police officers that were involved in the payoff system. There were first, the Chiefs of Police who during their respective tenures failed to exercise adequate controls to prevent the criminal activities of the officers. Secondly, there were the gamblers and homosexuals who paid off to the police to protect their own interests. Under the law, they are as guilty as the officers.... Thirdly, the Mayors and Councilmen in the past who conceived and perpetuated what was known as the

"tolerance policy" carried a major part of the responsibility for the shaping of conditions that spawned crime and corruption in the Seattle Police Department.

The report ended with a shrug:

> With the removal from the department of those officers known to have been involved, and the filing of criminal charges against several, the department through its own efforts has purged itself of most of the guilty officers. There are, of course, some officers who have not been exposed, so they will probably go unpunished, except by the knowledge of their guilt. Darkness, however, does not protect a man from his own conscience.

With this report, the Seattle Police Department washed its hands of the scandal. By then, Mayor Uhlman had found a new permanent chief from the small city of Garden Grove, California: George Tielsch. Tielsch had a reputation for personal incorruptibility. He immediately confirmed the policy initiated by Gain that Seattle police no longer accept gratuities, not even a cup of coffee. But Tielsch had no interest in further investigations. He arrived in office naked of any influence or friends in the SPD. His immediate goal was to win the backing of a rank and file buffeted by a year of turmoil. He told the *Call Box*, SPD's internal magazine:

> This police department has a lot to be proud of and nothing to be ashamed of. This department has had enough management by crisis. We've had too many quick changes and too many pseudo experts telling us what we need. [I promise no more] Monday morning quarter back game of determining what might have been.

Six months later, Tielsch claimed the department had already taken care of the problem:

> The frequent references to the past and present operation of the Seattle Police Department is disturbing. None of us appreciates the slightest reflection on the integrity of our department. . . . We can be secure and confident in the fact that we closed the door on the past. Our direction now is to continue our operation in a normal efficient manner, and plan for a very promising future.

With Tielsch in command, the SPD would not initiate any further housecleaning.

## King County's Prosecutor—Charles O. Carroll

With Stan Pitkin otherwise occupied and the SPD ready to move on, the only remaining investigating body was the King County prosecutor's office. In July 1970, Carroll cruised the Puget Sound in his yacht, occasionally reappearing in Seattle to issue a press release. During this period, Ed Heavey and I called for a county grand jury, as did the city council, bar associations, and some citizens' groups. All of us, though, openly doubted whether Carroll should lead it. It was only at the end of July, after he was done cruising, that Carroll responded to the clamor.

To the press, Carroll pointed out grand juries are expensive and the ongoing SPD task force investigation might make one unnecessary, but if a grand jury was needed, he would run it himself. That idea proved so unpopular that Carroll then proposed he'd find someone else to serve as a special prosecutor, the appointment to be approved by a majority of superior court judges.

Meanwhile, Carroll initiated a few obvious prosecutions. On July 31, Carroll filed a charge of felony bribery against Roy Hull, one of the police officers implicated by David Jessup in the Cook trial. On August 19, he filed two charges of bribery against David Devine, another officer. Finally, on August 28, he filed grafting charges against officers Jay Brozovich, Gerald Barmann, Wesley Youngquist, and a few days later, Ralph Zottman. Barmann had been one of the government's witnesses who testified against Cook, a fact noted by fellow police officers assessing whether to come clean themselves.

By the eve of the September primary, Carroll had taken the minimal steps needed for appearances while preserving his freedom to allow matters to slide later. If he had won the primary, the few prosecutions he initiated would have amounted to little, and he would have controlled a future grand jury, either directly or through a proxy.

But minimal as it had been, Carroll's zeal disappeared completely after he lost the primary. The deputies Carroll assigned to prosecute his bribery cases were his least experienced. Marco Magnano, fresh out of law school, recalls the Roy Hull bribery charge as in fact his first case ever. The grafting charges were misdemeanors, not felonies, with a one-year statute of limitations, but the incidents alleged dated back at least two years to 1968 and before. As the courts sorted out that mess, Carroll's deputies consistently recommended as much leniency as possible. And after the primary, Carroll brought no more prosecutions.

Before saying good-bye to Carroll the prosecutor, I should note one of Carroll's last acts in office. He invited me to his office in November and offered to put me on his payroll until I took office in January. He claimed it would be justified by the work I'd do coordinating the transition.

I refused.

## A Prophet is Not Without Honor, Save in His Own Land

Something else happening that summer and fall that compromised our later efforts: key prosecution witnesses fell from grace in the Seattle Police Department. During the Cook trial, the most effective testimony came from high-ranking officers like Tony Gustin, George Fuller, David Jessup, and Milton Price, who could credibly describe the corrupt conduct of fellow police. But before nine months had passed, all four would be demoted, fired, or pressured into retirement.

Assistant Chief George Fuller retired at the end of July, under pressure. He told the press he understood any new police chief coming in would need to make his own decisions regarding retention of assistant chiefs. Fuller preferred to leave immediately, so his retirement benefits would be tied to his current higher salary instead of the lower grade he expected after demotion. Fuller acknowledged that because of his role in the Palace Revolt and in testifying for Pitkin, he had become unpopular in the department.

On July 31, Tony Gustin, the hero of the Lifeline Club raid, was demoted by Gain from assistant chief to major and put in charge of the tactical squad, which constituted only a small part of his previous division. In succeeding years, Gustin would be moved to the juvenile division and later to a precinct command in Seattle's "Siberia"—Georgetown. While in Georgetown, he initiated an innovative team-policing concept only to be quickly transferred to the records department (and replaced in Georgetown by one of the officers prosecuted for assisting with graft). He retired from the SPD in 1977 and later commented they could have held his retirement party in a telephone booth.

Major David Jessup was fired in August. In his trial testimony, he had admitted to taking payoffs as part of his solo and quixotic efforts to uncover the payoff system. Acting Chief Toothman decided the testimony demonstrated behavior unbecoming to a police officer. Pitkin later hired Jessup to join him at the US attorney's office.

And near the end of August, Lieutenant Milton Price, the second-highest-ranking black officer on the force, was given a choice: retire or be terminated. He had taken bribes for a year, from 1960 to 1961, and testified voluntarily. The SPD was kind enough to delay the retirement until after Price vested at twenty years of service.

The active officers of the SPD saw the writing on the wall: lying to a grand jury might put you in legal trouble, but telling the truth put you in career trouble. The safest thing to do was to say as little as possible.

## Convening a Grand Jury

After I took office, I immediately asked for a grand jury. The superior court judges had formally voted to do this back on September 17, 1970, but wanted a new prosecutor in office before putting the measure into action. I requested a $150,000 budget from the county council, and after some haggling, they made a down payment of $50,000. In February, I got the additional $100,000, but only on a 5–4 vote (with Ed Heavey in the majority).

I formed a team of attorneys and investigators who would do the spadework and prosecute indictments over the next two and a half years. I would spend little time in trial on these criminal cases, though I did argue some of the many appeals. My main involvement was strategic and political, hiring the lead attorneys, determining the larger goals of the grand jury, and running interference between the litigation team and other government bodies, such as the Seattle Police Department. My goal was to make clear to my grand jury team and the public that the investigation would not be altered or obstructed by favoritism and courthouse politics. Early on, some of the grand jury targets, important people in local politics, would send their lawyers to my office saying their client was *not* going to run the television gauntlet and appear for questioning—why not just take a deposition? I told them their clients could always take the back stairs.

I was sometimes asked why I did not try the cases myself. I responded my main job was reforming the entire office. Trying high-profile cases would have shortchanged that, plus the fact that other public officials were involved would lead to charges that the whole exercise was political. Additionally, though I did not discuss this publicly, I had virtually no litigation experience. The whole "not trying cases" business came up in my 1974 reelection campaign, when my opponent ran an ad with an empty chair labeled "Prosecuting Attorney" in the courtroom. I finally struck upon an easily understood answer to this image conundrum: having the prosecuting attorney try cases was like having a police chief make arrests.

We rented space in the Smith Tower in Pioneer Square for the grand jury staff and deliberately kept them separate from the rest of the office. One of our difficulties at the time was that while the grand jury staff was probing past conduct within the SPD, my deputy prosecutors were working closely with the same department to develop and try current cases. To maintain confidence and a good working relationship, the criminal deputies had to be able to tell their police colleagues they didn't know anything about what was going on over in the Smith Tower.

The initial grand jury team included Doug Jewett and Evan Schwab and was led by Richard "Dick" McBroom, with Chief Criminal Deputy David Boerner providing liaison and oversight. Stan Pitkin had recruited McBroom from Ohio and put him to work on the federal grand jury, along with his brother Doug McBroom, who stayed behind with Pitkin when we hired Dick.

Security was a concern from the start. Seafirst bank provided a safekeeping vault in the bottom of the Dexter Horton Building. We bought a Hound Dog electronic device to sweep the office for bugs each night. At an early meeting, the word went out to everyone to be wary of using the phones—to simply assume they were bugged.

## Grand Old Juries

Grand juries are an old system for investigating crimes and official misdeeds and initiating prosecutions. The institution began in medieval England, when twelve to twenty-three citizens were called together for an extended period to look at evidence and decide whether charges were warranted. "Grand" refers to the greater number of jurors than in a "petit" trial jury of twelve, but the real difference was in function: a grand jury indicts and a petit jury tries cases. The Fifth Amendment specifies the federal government can charge crimes only through a grand jury. Unlike other rights contained in the Bill of Rights, this guarantee has not been applied to the states. Thus, in Washington, the grand jury's role in starting prosecutions by indictment had been supplanted by county prosecutors doing so by information, on their sole authority. But in 1971, state laws still made the county grand jury the *only* means of obtaining evidence by subpoena. Everyone recognized a grand jury is an unwieldy method of investigation, and our office pushed to make subpoena power available without the expense and publicity of a grand jury. Later in 1971, the legislature authorized superior courts to appoint a special inquiry judge with subpoena power when the local prosecutor needed that tool.

Theoretically, the grand jury moves the political weight of a charging decision off the shoulders of a prosecutor. A grand jury can decide for itself which subpoenas to issue or witnesses to hear, and a grand jury takes its own vote on who to indict. But in practice, the public and press treat a grand jury as an extension of the prosecutor. Sol Wachtler, a justice of New York's highest court, once said prosecutors could, if they wished, convince a grand jury to "indict a ham sandwich."

Because grand juries were infrequent, we had to invent procedures as we went along. Everybody knew that up on the eighth floor of the County Courthouse, police and politicians were being ushered into a room to be questioned regarding corruption and that someday indictments might emerge. But in order to protect witnesses and those targets who were never charged, all the testimony was kept secret. We tried to slip witnesses in by use of back elevators, to reduce scrutiny, but the press was pretty good at staking out locations at garage entrances and back entrances to get photographs, as well as catching the witnesses as they left.

This was the first grand jury convened since 1966 (the one called by Carroll to investigate courthouse renovations and a coincidental assessor bribery scandal) and only the fourth in the previous thirty years. Thus, there was a backlog of scandals and concerns people wanted investigated apart from police and municipal corruption. We were able to tackle some side issues but inevitably left many frustrated by not investigating everything. Because a wide-ranging grand jury had been so long awaited, and so often called for, it had also become the subject of great expectations. In theory, a grand jury that produces no indictments has still done its duty. In reality, if that had happened, I would have been condemned for wasting everybody's time and money.

## The Grand Jury Convenes—
## Kerfuffles Commence

The first grand jury session took place from April 13 to 19 and was devoted to the police payoff system. At jury selection, everyone noticed the attendance of SPD intelligence agents, who refused to tell intrigued journalists why they were there.

But it was outside the grand jury room that trouble with the SPD really started. Of the original three members of the Palace Guard, only Eugene Corr remained an assistant chief. Prior to the grand jury's beginning, Dick McBroom asked Corr for a reference on a potential investigator. Corr made the mistake of trying to help us out without clearing it with Chief Tielsch. When Tielsch discovered one of his officers had spoken to our staff without his permission, he blew up.

Tielsch demoted Corr for insubordination, reducing him two ranks to captain. (On hearing this, the head of the police officers' guild, George Berger, congratulated Tielsch for "weeding out incompetency.") Corr responded by retiring on April 2. A few days later, SPD sent the prosecutor's office a request to file a charge against Corr for borrowing seventy-six dollars from the police officers' association without paying it back—*back in 1966*. Because the charge alleged police corruption, we referred it to the grand jury, which summoned Tielsch to appear for forty-five minutes of questioning, mostly pressing him on why the police were going after Corr. When he got back to his office, Tielsch called my assistant and burned up the phone line with invective about how he had been mistreated by the grand jury, including claiming the witness stool had been raised so high that his feet couldn't touch the floor, a form of torture.

154 | SEATTLE JUSTICE

The grand jury refused to act against Corr, calling the charge "frivolous and malicious." There followed a quick war of press releases. Tielsch, backed up by Mayor Uhlman, labeled the entire grand jury a political enterprise. I responded, with as much equanimity as I could muster, that I had confidence in the police department and that the grand jury was completely not political. Oh, and by the way, the dreaded chair of torture was adjustable. (A member of the grand jury later gave me a thumbscrew. I kept it displayed on my desk.)

Tielsch had other reasons to be upset at the grand jury. Eager to secure duty rosters and other departmental records, we served Tielsch at his office with a subpoena for records, without a heads-up. Tielsch felt personally offended by the lack of warning. But as one of the prosecutors, Doug Jewett, noted, we did not really want to give the police warning that there were particular records we were looking for. They might have mysteriously disappeared.

The Corr episode made it clear a contingent inside SPD would treat any officer helping to expose the payoff system as a traitor, and Tielsch would go along with it. Gustin, Fuller, Jessup, Price, and now Corr: the highest-ranking officers who had revolted against a corrupt system had all been demoted, fired, or forced to retire.

I knew Tielsch and I had to patch things up. Forget the grand jury—police and prosecutors must work closely together for normal criminal cases to proceed. We decided on lunch at Ray's Boathouse. This turned into a most friendly two-martini affair, at the end of which Tielsch invited me to go for a spin in the police helicopter. I recall he had a police driver for his ride to the helipad next to Gas Works Park, but I was on my own in the Brown Bomber, a giant 1967 Pontiac Chuck Carroll had left me. We set off on a whirl over the skies of Seattle while my staff back in the office wondered why I hadn't returned from the reconciliation lunch. I can't remember any angry phone calls from George Tielsch after that, though our relationship never became very close.

Until the principal indictments came, the most interesting grand jury episode was a brief sideshow involving envelopes filled with cash, totaling $2,500, left on Mayor Uhlman's desk for two months running in the summer of 1970 by persons unknown. The mystified mayoral staff put the money into a safe and asked the police to investigate, a matter only made public after some pointed questions by the press working off of confidential tips. The grand jury obtained a brief appearance by Uhlman, but the mystery of who placed the money there, and why, remained unresolved.

Indictments were slow at first. The grand jury filed five indictments in May, against two police officers, a sheriff's lieutenant, a liquor board inspector, and a local criminal attorney. In June came only two more indictments, against another two police officers. By July 23, Ed Donohoe, editor of the *Washington Teamster*, and not a particular friend of reform, pronounced the grand jury a "rancid turkey."

But near the end of July, after four months of deliberation, the grand jury charged eleven more individual policemen. Then on July 27 came the indictment for which the jury will be chiefly remembered: a charge that nineteen SPD leaders and high political figures, including former prosecutor Carroll, former sheriff Jack Porter, and former chief Ramon, had joined in a conspiracy to defraud the Seattle public through the police payoff system and the Tolerance Policy. Our goal was to include as many as possible in the network of officials who maintained Seattle's payoff system.

The legal definition of a conspiracy is an agreement by parties to accomplish illegal acts, or legal acts by illegal means. It can be charged separately from any underlying crimes. A prosecutor does not need to prove all parties agreed at the same time or even that they all agreed with each other so long as the agreement itself could be proved. Nor need he show each participant in the conspiracy committed an illegal act—only that each was part of the agreement and one of the group took a substantial step to carry out such an act. The substantial step need not itself be illegal—if you agreed to rob a bank with several others, the step could be simply buying masks. All this meant that if we could prove Carroll and others agreed to protect the payoff system, we could get a conviction even if Carroll did not accept payoffs.

But conspiracy charges require proof of an agreement and that a particular defendant joined the agreement. Because direct proof of an agreement is difficult, our evidence consisted mostly of showing coordinated actions. It was relatively easy to prove low-level police officers exacted payoffs from businessmen. It was much harder to show higher-level officials and politicians assisted and protected the payoffs or associated bribery schemes.

A conspiracy trial against nineteen people saved the time and expense of separate trials but also meant confronting the combined resources of nineteen savvy defense attorneys. Whether or not they conspired beforehand, during litigation the conspiracy defendants effectively coordinated their actions.

One problem we also faced was that conspiracy indictments are controversial in themselves, as they come close to criminalizing associations. We saw this attitude in the reaction of Michael Rosen, a friend of Dave Boerner's and an ACLU attorney who fully supported our tackling corruption. On the day the indictment was announced, Rosen encountered Boerner on the street, congratulated him on hearing the news, and asked the form of charge. When Boerner replied "conspiracy," Rosen's jaw dropped and he said he could not support that. Shortly thereafter, pressured by the national organization, the local ACLU office called on me to drop the conspiracy charge and bring individual indictments.

Regardless of the form it came in, some of Old Seattle was simply outraged by the indictment itself and its attack on the cherished hypocrisy of Seattle's Tolerance Policy. Ed Donohoe, as usual, expressed himself vividly. The grand jury, he said, had obeyed the instructions of the "arch-conspirators"—me, Pitkin, and Gorton—to smear the police department, sheriffs, and political office holders. Why, asked Ed, "didn't they indict Pope Paul and all the Seattle flock who ever played a game of bingo just to keep the parochial grade schools open?"

## The Perils of an Open Bar

After the conspiracy indictment, the grand jury remained in session through September, but with one exception, those sessions were anticlimactic. That was the indictment of all three members of the Washington State Liquor Control Board.

This is a tangent from the other grand jury cases, but it's worth describing if only to demonstrate our determination to follow up on criminal activity regardless of political fallout. I turned out to be Governor Evans's most insubordinate puppet.

The liquor board is appointed by the governor, and by this time in 1971, all three members were Evans appointees. The board was powerful because liquor could be sold only through restaurants, taverns, and state-owned liquor stores, which operated subject to numerous constraints even after voters ended the blue laws in 1966.

Witnesses testifying about the payoff system stated liquor-control inspectors had participated. Inspectors took their own payoffs (twenty dollars and all the free drinks they could survive were common), plus helped the police maintain the payoff system by strictly enforcing liquor laws on recalcitrant bar owners. One inspector was indicted in June, but in the course of investigation, the grand jury turned up another problem—the liquor board itself was making free with the samples held in the state's warehouses.

These samples were ostensibly provided to the board for tests of safety or flavor so the board could determine which brands to stock. But the board treated these samples as their private supply, for their own use or for political favors, and sometimes simply commandeered liquor from suppliers unilaterally. In 1969 alone, 305 cases of liquor went unaccounted for, all of which were major brands, not new or marginal offerings.

Even more ticklish was the connection to the governor's mansion. The liquor board provided office holders with alcohol for parties, most prominently the governor's Christmas bash. The practice began prior to Evans but continued during his administration. Prosecution of the liquor board would necessarily embarrass the man who was my political mentor and hero.

Despite all this, I don't think the liquor board indictment would have caused significant ill will with the governor if we hadn't made a big mistake in how we informed him. I should have called Dan Evans or his chief of staff, Jim Dolliver, directly with a heads-up but instead asked my aide Richard Allison to call Dolliver, whom he barely knew and did not connect with. Politicians don't like to get their news from the papers, but that's where Evans heard his liquor board was being indicted.

Evans handled himself well when confronted by the press, proclaiming a desire to find out the truth of the allegations while reiterating the point that guilt could not be presumed. But at the next spring's political roast, I had to watch while Mayor Uhlman went on an extended routine mocking my friend the governor, including handing a nearly empty fifth to an unamused Evans.

## October Surprise, December Tragedy

Following the indictments, we put together a schedule of trials, hoping to work our way through the individual cases in the fall and winter of 1971, leaving the conspiracy trial for the end. We assigned experienced deputies, who of course had been in the office under Carroll. Ironically, many of the excellent criminal attorneys opposing us, including Anthony Savage, J. Emmet Walsh, and Joel Rindal, had also served under Carroll. They filed pretrial motions seeking dismissal of the charges on a wide range of technical grounds. Because so many of the King County judges had connections with the defendants, Judge William Cole was brought in from Kittitas County to hear the motions. On October 20, he dismissed the conspiracy case on the grounds that (1) the state's conspiracy statute was unconstitutional and (2) the enactment of a new grand jury statute on May 10, 1971, invalidated any decision made by the already impaneled jury after that date.

The latter ruling was an example of good intentions gone awry. Anticipating the need for a grand jury, in early 1971, we lobbied in Olympia for changes to grand jury laws that would make them more usable—for example, barring attorneys from being present with witnesses. The amended grand jury law was enacted on May 10, 1971, a month after the grand jury convened. To be on the safe side, Judge Stanley Soderland, who oversaw the grand jury, reswore the jury members. Nevertheless, Judge Cole found the effect of the changes to the law was to invalidate our existing grand jury.

Judge Cole's ruling floored us. At the time, I was in Eastern Washington speaking to a Republican audience about the case with all the optimism of ignorance. I promised the press an immediate appeal, but the Washington Supreme Court operates on its own schedule. It was two months, until December 20, before I argued the appeal before the court and another seven long months, until

August 1972, before the court unanimously reversed Judge Cole's decision, making short shrift of his ruling:

> Truly, indeed, to hold the King County grand jury ceased to exist in the evening hours of May 10, 1971, would be against good common sense and would be against the interests of society. It would be the kind of thing that causes the public at large to lose confidence in law. We do not so hold.

After so many months of waiting, the words were of little comfort. The defense immediately sought a rehearing, and the Supreme Court did not reject that motion until October 1972. All told, Cole's decision in October 1971 cost us a year. The delay killed momentum. Cooperation from the street and police witnesses dried up, and trial team morale sagged. Even worse, the team leader was struck down shortly after the Cole dismissal.

Dick McBroom, the prosecutor we recruited from Pitkin to lead the grand jury, became sick in November 1971 and by December 3 had to take leave. Incredibly, only nine days later he was dead, the victim of a rare blood disease at the age of twenty-nine. Up to his last days, he worked hard and stayed late, trying to win cooperation from witnesses.

Dick McBroom's death was a personal loss to all of us. It also threw a wrench in our plans for prosecution. We delayed the impending trial of a jail guard who sold hacksaws to prisoners, and in January, I selected Marco Magnano, Ron Clark, and Jack Cunningham to head the special trials section along with the remaining attorneys. We scrambled to regroup and, while waiting for the supreme court to rule on the conspiracy case, take care of what trials we could.

## Treading Water

While most of the indictments were on hold, we were able to try those few defendants indicted before May 10. One example illustrated the tough road ahead. In February 1972, we brought Officer Ellsworth Robinson to trial on four counts of bribery. Witness MacIver Wells and others testified Robinson had taken cash payoffs, as well as liquor. But despite two years of headlines about police corruption, the police rank and file still remained popular with the public. The jury found him guilty but then sent a note to the judge saying it was only for taking free drinks. Commendably, Judge Francis Walterskirchen sentenced Robinson to a minimum of a year in prison and a maximum of ten, commenting a citizenry must have confidence in its officers. Few subsequent judges would prove so severe.

A particular disappointment later in 1972 was the sentence given to Rudy Santos for perjury. Santos, head of the Filipino Social and Improvement Club, provided substantial payoffs to the police and refused to cooperate with the grand jury. We asked for five years, hoping a significant sentence for perjury would motivate other witnesses not to lie during trial. Judge Fred Dore gave Santos a suspended sentence. And, he said, he saw no reason for probation.

In 1972, while waiting for news from Olympia, I asked deputies Magnano, Clark, and Cunningham to flesh out knowledge of the payoff system by interviewing more police officers and bar owners. We learned interesting new details. Graft was not limited to the urban core; payoffs were also reported from University District and Lake City businesses, though the money was never as substantial or consistent as that coerced from downtown locations. In Ballard, the chief source of payoff money turned out to be the Elks Lodge, a venue of substantial gambling.

The interviews further clarified the moral rot to be found within the department. One police officer was not content with waiting for monthly payoffs but also shook down drunks he found in Pioneer Square. His partner watched him take wallets to check IDs, remove any cash, and return the wallets. The partner refused a share but did not report his colleague. Some of the victims tried to complain to duty sergeants. They were ignored.

And then there were stories that came out of left field. At the end of an interview otherwise devoted to payoffs, one policeman spontaneously inquired, "Is there any statute of limitations for murder?" His interrogators inquired whether he had killed anybody. No, he said, he was thinking about an incident ten years before, when he had been one of several policemen appearing at a crime scene. A woman lay dying, after falling six stories from the window of the apartment of her boyfriend, a former deputy prosecutor and later an attorney for Frank Colacurcio. The policeman observed bruising on the victim's arm and scratch marks on the window frame in the apartment, indicating she probably got pushed out the window and hadn't jumped out, as claimed by the boyfriend. But his sergeant had told him to stop his inquiries. And since so many years had passed, my office didn't pursue it.

## Back in the Field

After the supreme court reversed Judge Cole's decision, we scored some successes in individual trials, but again sentences were light. By the end of 1972, we were mostly preparing for the conspiracy trial. One of King County's most experienced jurists, James W. Mifflin, was selected to try the conspiracy case. We had wanted a younger judge, like David Soukup, who did not know most of the defendants. Also alarming was that Judge Mifflin was the unanimous choice of defense attorneys. We asked Mifflin to recuse himself, but he refused, noting he had ruled against us with regard to liquor board warrants the previous year and we should have objected then. I met with him personally and could not get a change of mind, but he did assure me of his fairness. It was time to get this case tried, and we accepted a trial date of April 30.

By the end of 1972, the number of conspiracy defendants had been whittled down to seventeen. Charles Waitt, King County's business licensing manager, died in October 1971 after an illness. Henry Schultheis, a police major in charge of the North Precinct, fled the country in July 1972. His last known address was a mobile home park in Puerto Peñasco, Mexico, where he could not be served, and it was not worth the expense and trouble of having him extradited.

I appointed Norm Maleng to lead the trial team. He had been the chief civil deputy, impressing everyone with his strategic skills, including helping to overcome legal challenges to the Kingdome, which was finally under construction in 1972. Norm would later become my distinguished successor, the longest serving King County prosecutor ever and one of the best.

Pretrial, Maleng was immediately faced with a rude surprise; on February 6, Mifflin dismissed six people from the conspiracy case. Mifflin combined two old Washington statutes to bathe grand jury witnesses in full immunity even when they did not claim that right during their testimony. This argument had been concocted by the distinguished Seattle attorney and future federal judge Bill Dwyer, who represented Councilmember Charles M. Carroll. Ironically, shortly before the court's decision, we realized the evidence against Councilmember Carroll was pretty thin and dismissed him from the case on our own motion, "in the interests of justice."

## The Conspiracy Faces Trial

Finally, in May of 1973, there came the trial. In a hundred years of city history, individual police officers had been convicted of graft. But never before had anybody tried a case predicated on the charge that individual officers were part of a larger corrupt system and that all who supported the system shared in the guilt of the payoffs. Time and time again, one heard that corrupt officers amounted to nothing more than a few rotten apples in a barrel. Our goal was to show it was the barrel itself that was rotten, tainting all the officers, good and bad, that it contained.

The task was ambitious. It wasn't just a question of providing more examples of fifty-dollar payoffs and free drinks. The conspiracy case sought to illuminate and convict the Tolerance Policy itself, a system of legalized vice openly defended by Seattle's political leaders for more than twenty years and with roots going back another eighty. Our trial memorandum put it this way:

> During the 1950's and 1960's King County and Seattle law enforcement officials, using the Seattle Police Department as their primary collection apparatus, operated an extensive payoff and extortion system that permeated nearly every facet of Seattle's night-life industry and generated a flow of illicit money measured in tens of thousands of dollars per month. Although this was a situation that traced its origins back to pre-depression times, the state will outline a payoff system that knew its most extensive and lucrative years under the control of the conspirators in this case....
>
> The state will outline during this case the backbone of the payoff system—the operation of gambling machines and cardrooms. Permitted under the guise of the so-called "tolerance policy," the state will show that local governmental

officials, in league with the Seattle Police Department, permitted open gambling in obvious violation of state law. The testimony will show there was a clear reason why this gambling was tolerated—because it supplied a steady flow of money to the politicians who endorsed it (publicly or privately) and into the highly organized payoff system existent in the Seattle Police Department....

Large payoffs were possible because of the profitability of the gambling tables. This profitability of the gambling tables was in turn a function of both the police payoff protection *and* the ostensible legitimacy of the operation under the so called "tolerance policy." This "legitimacy" permitted the largest gambling establishments to advertise and to operate publicly in obvious violation of state law. Thus the tolerance policy and the payoff system were integrally related—and dependent on each other.

Over four weeks of trial, we told our story. Particularly through former mayor Dorm Braman's testimony, we showed that the city officially embraced the Tolerance Policy. Police witnesses documented the extortion of funds from the bars and businesses subject to the Tolerance Policy, showing its corrosive effect.

But at trial we suffered from weak and hostile witnesses, plus what I think is fair to call the animus of the trial judge.

Our police witnesses were able to reinforce the point made in the Cook trial that there was an extensive system of police graft, reaching up to the highest levels of the police department. Unfortunately, witnesses who could tie the high-ranking members of the conspiracy to payoffs wilted under cross-examination. The worst example was former deputy sheriff Glenn York, then living in California. He had a juicy story to tell, which he had related to Lou

Guzzo of the *Seattle P-I* in 1968 and also before Pitkin's federal grand jury.

At trial, on May 10, York told the story again, describing a meeting in 1963 that included Prosecutor Carroll, Ben Cichy, and Chief Ramon at the office of York's boss, Sheriff Jack Porter. York testified Carroll proposed to Sheriff Porter that the county be opened up to pinball gambling just as the city was. Cichy gave Porter some money at the meeting and promised more. York testified that over succeeding weeks, he went to a local tavern and received more payoffs from Cichy to give to Porter.

Next morning's *P-I* headlines trumpeted the evidence that finally put Carroll in the middle of the corruption and payoffs. But that same day, Anthony Savage began his cross-examination and confirmed his reputation as one of Seattle's most effective criminal defense attorneys by pushing York into a classic witness meltdown.

The problem was that York's testimony to the grand jury differed from his testimony at trial. In the interim, York had changed details of the 1963 meeting—for example, who went in when. And for some reason, York told the grand jury that when he began serving as a sheriff's deputy there was little or no gambling in the county, but at trial, he testified there was gambling in the county in the early sixties. In and of themselves, the discrepancies were not highly significant, at least regarding what happened in the 1963 meeting with Cichy and Carroll. But faced with the differences, York fell apart. He let himself get pinned down by Savage's hostile questioning—was York lying when he made his previous statements to the county grand jury? A simple no would have worked, but York instead began equivocating on the stand as to what a lie consisted of and whether it was possible to lie about something without really meaning to, finally admitting at the excruciating end of his rambling answer that yes, under some definitions, he had lied.

One of our major goals had been to put the Tolerance Policy itself on trial by demonstrating how campaign contributions from gamblers encouraged politicians to tolerate gambling. One of the best-situated witnesses was former mayor Dorm Braman, but he was also one of the most reluctant.

Braman testified that in the spring of 1964, near the end of his mayoral campaign, he was running out of funds needed to pay for advertising. Carroll contacted Braman to tell him that certain police officers were collecting money for him on Skid Road and that Braman should avoid having any obligations to such lowlifes. Carroll then offered to connect Braman with money that would never make any demands on him and never whisper a word about obligations. Carroll delegated his longtime chief investigator, Marvin Stenholm, to take Braman on a road trip for cash. In one afternoon, the two stopped at four different locations to pick up contributions. Bob Murray, friend of Carroll and owner of the Dog House restaurant, handed over $500. Ben Cichy donated $1,000. Rudy Santos, head of the Filipino Social and Improvement Club and a known source of payoffs, paid another $500 as did Cal Decker, another restaurant owner.

There's a curious coda to this story, though it was not mentioned at the trial. A few weeks after making the rounds with Braman, Stenholm went on a fishing trip off Sekiu on the coast of the Olympic Peninsula and was lost at sea, presumed dead. Based on anonymous informants, the author William Chambliss claimed Stenholm was murdered because he developed a conscience and was considering revealing the corruption. There's even less evidence for this than for Cichy's untimely death in 1969, but both incidents became part of Seattle's underworld folklore of the time, proof those who might tell tales ended up underwater.

Braman also testified he told Carroll he was angry that the police, through their guild, were backing Lieutenant Governor

Cherberg in the mayoral race, in spite of Braman's previous support of unions. Shortly thereafter, Braman got $1,000 in cash from Assistant Chief Buzz Cook.

But if Braman told a supportive story on direct examination, he unleashed a diatribe on cross-examination, aimed squarely at the prosecution and me. He characterized the last-minute fund-raising as normal campaign contributions received from normal businessmen, denied any quid pro quo, and criticized the prosecution. And as he had all his life, he defended the Tolerance Policy for the usual reason—that it was needed to prevent organized crime. We faced a fundamental problem of convincing a skeptical judge that the openly created policy of tolerating illegal gambling could also be part of a criminal conspiracy. Overall, Braman's testimony may have helped the defendants.

By the time of trial, we were already wary of Judge Mifflin, given his decision to dismiss six defendants. We requested a jury, but Mifflin denied our motion. Only criminal defendants have a right to demand a jury, and all ten of the remaining defendants, to our surprise, agreed to waive jury rights. Apparently they liked the idea of Mifflin being both judge and jury.

At trial, our fears proved warranted. Mifflin openly discussed the weaknesses of our case from the bench. On the first day of the second week, he stated his displeasure with our legal theory, saying we should have charged bribery, not conspiracy. Mifflin was also open about his dislike for some of our witnesses, announcing at the end of York's fiasco that he simply put no credence in any of York's testimony. Nor, he told us, did he see campaign contributions as relevant parts of a conspiracy absent a quid pro quo bribe.

On May 17, defendants moved for dismissal, and that afternoon, Mifflin dismissed from the case Charles O. Carroll, Jack Porter, Ray Carroll, Ron Smith, Charles R. Connery, Robert Covach, Lee W. Scott, and W. W. Cook. All that were left were high-ranking police officers Buzz Cook and Lyle J. LaPointe. To make his action more final, Mifflin did not dismiss at the end of the state's case, which would have invited an appeal, but instead advised the defendants to rest their case too, and then dismissed afterward. Because his grounds included his assessment that our key witnesses were not credible, we would have had a tough time winning an appeal. A higher court rarely overrules a trial judge's decision regarding credibility.

Some of the prosecutors who were part of the grand jury team are still bitter about Mifflin, believing his long acquaintance with many of the defendants and their defense attorneys biased his decisions. On the other hand, another former prosecutor, Marco Magnano, told me he considered Mifflin an experienced judge who acted fairly. My view is that for whatever reason, Mifflin thought we brought a weak case and was determined to put a quick end to it.

Reviews in the press were not kind. Anthony Savage, in particular, took a carnivorous joy in discussing our defeat. He told the press we had been derelict, as anybody talking to Glenn York would know he was permanently out to lunch. Though deprived of most of its defendants, the trial was not over, and in the end, we eked out a small success. The trial resumed on May 21. Cook took the stand to stoutly deny being part of any scheme at all, LaPointe rested without testimony, and Mifflin found them both guilty of conspiracy.

Rendering his decision, Mifflin stated his only regret was that he did not have all those involved in the system before him, including those who made the payoffs. It was a curious point. In Mifflin's thinking, the guilt of those bar owners pressured into making payoffs was equal to the guilt of those who did the pressuring. It clearly pained Mifflin to convict any police officer in this case.

Mifflin sentenced LaPointe to a year in county jail and a five-year suspended sentence, commenting he got off lightly because he was no more guilty than the witnesses against him and had

demonstrated honor by "not ratting on the other rats." Mifflin
gave Cook the same sentence and recommended both for work
release. Actual confinement, Mifflin commented, would just cost
the county money.

## Odds and Ends and the Judgment of History

If this were a play, the conspiracy decision would be the dramatic
finale, but in reality, trials of perjury and bribery cases against individual officers dragged on for nearly another year, into 1974. Ultimately, we secured several more guilty pleas from officers in return
for light sentences and resignations.

Meanwhile we worked with the police department to do further
internal purges. Our goal had been to punish key figures in the payoff system, but absent that, we wanted at least to get corrupt officers
out of the force. Starting in January 1973, we began providing Chief
Tielsch with summaries of all damaging testimony available with
respect to police still on active duty, as collected by the grand juries,
task force, and our investigators. We had evidence that approximately half of active duty captains and large numbers of lieutenants
and sergeants had at some point taken an active role in the payoff
system. By the summer of 1973, we had turned over all that we had,
and Tielsch took over discipline. In addition to our prosecutions,
his department forced another thirteen police officers to resign.

During the course of contacts with Tielsch's staff, my deputies
were informed, in no uncertain terms, that the police officers' guild
would go after me in the coming election because the rank and file
hated my guts. They felt I applied a lower standard of guilt to police
officers caught up in payoffs than I did to ordinary criminals, and
like Judge Mifflin, they felt I erred by going after police officers
accepting bribes rather than the card room operators paying them.

My office worked hard that summer to reestablish good relationships with the police department, because, in the end, prosecutors and police must work together to prevent crimes and catch criminals. I don't know that I ever became much loved by the Seattle police, but there were few blowups, and the threat to take me down in 1974 never turned into anything significant.

The actual finale is, all in all, unsatisfying. In total, the grand jury indicted fifty-five people. One fled to Mexico and two died (one by his own hand), but of the fifty-two remaining, we only convicted twenty. Inevitably, in every assessment of my reelection chances, observers would begin by noting the grand jury and its allegedly paltry results. In early 1974, Herb Robinson of the *Times* called the grand jury a "fizzle."

The length of the proceedings and the long delays in litigation did have one beneficial side effect, at least for my political future—people had grown weary of the scandal and wanted to move on. The last of the grand jury convictions and sentencing occurred in the spring of 1974, just in time to not intrude on my reelection. Even those who found my efforts inadequate had positive things to say about the other work of the prosecutor's office. For many people, the great payoff scandal of 1970 had become a vague memory of something unpleasant that had happened in the ever-receding past. In his history of Seattle, *Seattle: Past to Present*, written in the late '70s, Roger Sale discusses many topics, right up to the Boeing Bust of 1970 and the cultural renaissance of the 1970s. He never mentions the payoffs or Charles O. Carroll or the grand jury and its indictments.

Looking back, our legal and tactical missteps are reasonably clear. We didn't anticipate Judge Cole's interpretation of the new grand jury law. We should not have allowed people we intended to indict to testify before the grand jury. At various steps along the way, we alienated Chief Tielsch by not giving him insights into where our investigation was going. To say the least, Glenn York's witness preparation could have used some more time. There were other things over which we had less control, such as Richard McBroom's untimely death or the supreme court's eight-month delay on deciding the validity of the grand jury. I also believe trial court judges Cole and Mifflin made some questionable legal decisions. Ultimately, the goal itself was a difficult one, and a prosecutor's case is no stronger than its evidence. We had little incriminating documentation or wiretaps. We depended on our witnesses, and few police officers, bar owners, or others involved wanted to testify against people they liked or feared. The few became fewer over three and a half years of federal and county litigation and delay.

Ultimately, showing that figures like Chief Ramon, Sheriff Porter, and above all, Prosecutor Carroll were part of a large-scale conspiracy against the public interest required people to find criminal that which they had come to think of as simply normal politics in the Queen City, part of Seattle's everyday life. Carroll was not stupid, and there's little evidence he was personally greedy. There may exist better evidence than we found of his connections to police payoffs, but it remained hidden in the memories of recalcitrant or absent witnesses.

My own opinion is that Carroll took money from gamblers not for personal gain but for power—to get reelected and to donate money to other politicians and judges as campaign contributions. He tolerated the Tolerance Policy for the same reason other politicians did: to preserve a system that worked for him. He ignored the accusations of payoffs because investigations would have caused trouble and upset that system. I think he was corrupt but not in a manner easily identifiable as criminal.

So I understand the view that the grand jury was a fizzle, a failure. But I disagree. The indictments were only partly successful, but they were worth doing, in fact essential. They completed a job that

Stan Pitkin and George Tielsch had left unfinished, and cauterized a culture of graft that could have easily returned.

We did not get every conviction. But we did improve the world we found on January 1, 1971. Policemen predisposed to coerce citizens into giving bribes were jailed or forced into resignations. There have been cases of bribery or graft against individual officers since then, but nothing approaching the payoff system has ever reemerged. The laws regarding campaign contributions became more restrictive, and disclosure rules more stringent. Big money still influences local elections today, more so than ever. But the surreptitious provision of cash is at least more likely to be exposed. As Rick Anderson, author of *Seattle Vice*, told me recently, what we accomplished was to publicly name the actors in Seattle's conspiracy of corruption. Seattle, in its way, has always been something of a small town. Once the principal actors in the web were named and their means of operation were exposed, it was difficult for anyone to think of putting something similar back in place again.

Seattle's hundred-year experiment in hypocrisy and selective enforcement corrupted everybody it touched. The grand jury made the choice painfully clear—legalize vice or prosecute it. Seattle was ready to go straight. And that included the police department.

Shortly after helping Norm Maleng try the conspiracy case, Deputy Prosecutor Marco Magnano took a one-month position evaluating the prosecuting attorney's juvenile division. This required trips up to the juvenile detention facility on the other side of First Hill, a long uphill walk. One day as he was headed back to the courthouse, a police car drove up with two young officers inside. They asked him if he had been one of the prosecutors on the conspiracy case. When Magnano admitted he had been, they invited him in for a ride downtown, an offer he accepted somewhat warily. During the ride, they thanked him for helping to clean up the department. They'd hated the payoff system and were glad it was gone.

## Second Time Around

The election of 1970 had been like climbing a mountain: all absorbing. After four years in office, my reelection in 1974 held less drama. My opponent again was Ed Heavey, but for him the second time around was probably a little less exhilarating. His near win in 1970 kept him interested in the office, but he was not able to raise much money, and as the filing date approached in August of 1974, he had seemed to give up on the idea. But then, at the last minute, he acquired a powerful patron.

In 1974, venerable senator Warren "Maggie" Magnuson ran for reelection. Maggie's power in the Senate was near its peak, but his old age left him vulnerable at home. As filing approached, there was a wave of speculation that Slade Gorton might run against him. The Democrats worried that if I had no opposition, the "Bayley machine" would help Gorton. So to keep me busy, Maggie promised Heavey $10,000 to run for prosecutor, enough to finally entice him into the race.

Heavey tried very hard. We overlearned the lesson of the last election and did little campaigning before the primary, husbanding our money for the final. Heavey spoke everywhere he could and even managed to advertise, although the ads may not have helped much. Some of them tried to tie me to the red-hot Watergate scandal, an implausible connection that left Heavey's campaign looking a little shabby.

In the primary, Heavey got over 40 percent of the vote. Afterward, with the invaluable help of Cam Hall, who joined up as campaign manager, I went after Heavey with more vigor. At the first debate of the final, I pointed out he was getting financial support from some of the same gamblers I had recently indicted or convicted for gambling and corruption. Our reward was photos of Heavey, red faced, pointing his finger at me and sputtering.

Magnuson's support for Heavey went little further than paying him to get in the race, and Washington's other powerful Democratic senator was no help either. When he heard that Senator Henry "Scoop" Jackson would be at the Olympic Hotel in October to hold a press conference, Heavey arrived with a camera crew and reserved a room to shoot a TV ad with Scoop. But Jackson dodged the opportunity, leaving Heavey hanging with his camera crew in front of a pack of amused journalists.

On election night, November 5, 1974, I had some reasons to worry about the result: peripheral fallout from Watergate, angry police officers, general disappointment at the grand jury results, running as a Republican in an increasingly Democratic county, and memories of the 1970 nail-biter. But the trepidations and butterflies went to bed early that night, as did I. I won again, this time by 78,439 votes. It was my last electoral victory.

# CHAPTER 7

# JUSTICE

★ ★ ★ ★ ★ ★ ★ ★ ★ ★ ★ ★

## Starting Fresh

While the work of the grand jury was playing out over my first term, my more basic concern in the prosecutor's office was to wrench it from its political and partisan rut.

Carroll was prosecutor for twenty-two years and in his time perfected the Power Model of a prosecutor's office; he used his position to maximize his own professional and political power, which radiated down through police departments and out to judges, other politicians, and local party stalwarts. For those who worked in Carroll's office, politics was omnipresent. During the 1964 mayoral campaign, Carroll called all his staff deputies and secretaries into a room to meet candidate Dorm Braman and be told he was the candidate to support. As one former prosecutor who served under Carroll noted, even his office Christmas parties were political, for the focus was on the party politicians who were invited, not the prosecutors who served. In 1970, two recently hired prosecutors, Marco Magnano and Ron Clark, were pressed into campaign service, which involved sign making, sign distribution, and doorbelling. Clark vividly recalls such duties took priority over work:

I remember being out at District Court and being called to go to a warehouse where they were making yard signs for Carroll. After I got there, somebody asked me where I had parked my car, which was a county car. I said out front. They told me move the car. Later that night I was driving around with Pat Harber [later Pat Aiken], putting up signs. For me it was all Courthouse politics.

I wanted to develop a different model—what I eventually came to call the Justice Model. I consciously tried to reduce the personal power of the prosecutor while extending the scope of the office itself. We looked for opportunities to rectify injustice, bring a rule of law to places neglected before, and make justice itself the guiding principle, not political influence or partisan benefit. I did not want to be a better political boss than Carroll; I wanted the office to move outside of the political world.

## Putting on the Blindfolds

In one respect starting fresh was easy—Carroll cleaned out his office before he left. On January 11, 1971, I walked into a large office with a very large and empty desk. Hinting at Carroll's interview techniques, the lower right-hand drawer of his desk had a hole cut in the back with a tangle of unconnected wires once attached, I had no doubt, to a tape recorder. Carroll's top deputies had also left, leaving empty drawers and empty folders. All office manuals had been removed, as well as administrative files and personnel records. Mostly the office contained the remaining lower-level deputy prosecutors, some perhaps worried about their jobs. Like Carroll, I was a Republican, but everyone knew I was an Evans Republican, of a different faction than Carroll, and these factions had been battling in local politics for six years. Would I replace Carroll's people with Evans loyalists?

But changing the culture did not mean firing existing deputies—in fact, the opposite. I saw no need to make significant changes in the staff I found in the courthouse. Carroll's deputies were generally professional and could be counted on to competently try the cases Carroll deigned to take on. If nothing else, Carroll knew the electoral value of hiring competent people. To the extent Carroll had unsavory agendas, those were matters he kept to himself and his closest deputies. Unless a case brushed up against one of Carroll's political preoccupations, prosecutors were free to call their cases as they saw them. In fact, as one said later, they saw very little of "the Old Man," and his only feedback on their work was occasional notes, often harsh, written with the green ink Carroll reserved for his use.

I named David Boerner, an avowed Democrat, my chief criminal deputy. I sent him around the offices to talk with the remaining staff, evaluate their qualities, and reassure them they were not about to be fired or required to swear loyalty to me or to a party. In the end, we retained everybody in the criminal division and promoted some to leadership. Boerner's tour did result in one major change. When he returned, he told me Patricia Harber, one of the few female deputies, should be made assistant chief criminal deputy.

## Playing Favorites

Early on, I tried to make clear the office would make charging decisions in high-profile cases without concern for political repercussions. The grand jury indictments were one extended example, but there were other opportunities. Early in 1971, Dave Boerner was in a car with two Renton police detectives and listened while they discussed a conversation between a murder suspect and his attorney.

Boerner quickly realized the only possible source was an intercepted or recorded attorney-client communication. We charged Renton's captain of detectives with illegal eavesdropping, which was both the right thing to do and a good legal move, preempting objections by the murder defendant's lawyer. It also probably represented a departure from previous practice, as Carroll was never known for prosecuting cops.

A smaller thing that had even greater impact was the Cle Elum phone call. In the middle of the night, a brand new deputy named Bill Fligeltaub received a phone call from police stating that they had picked up the mayor of Cle Elum on a drunk-driving charge. The police wanted to know what to do. Fligeltaub quickly replied to treat the mayor like anybody else then went back to sleep. I appeared at the next 7:30 a.m. staff meeting specifically to tell the deputy he had done the right thing, in front of everybody else. The principle was clear and the word spread.

## A New Attitude

In my campaign, I frequently criticized Carroll for being too cautious in bringing prosecutions. He avoided bringing criminal cases he was not guaranteed to win. Ed Donohoe, the Teamsters' curmudgeon journalist, nicknamed all Seattle politicians who amounted to anything. I was the "Doe-Eyed Prosecutor," Dan Evans was "Straight Arrow," and Wes Uhlman was "Greytop." Early on, Donohoe dubbed Chuck Carroll "Fair Catch," referring to his caution. Police relayed to me their frustration when they would bring the prosecutor what they thought were good cases, only to have Carroll refuse to bring charges. For example, Carroll had a rule: any robbery case required two witnesses, otherwise there'd be no prosecution.

Caution is not per se bad. A criminal charge disrupts the life of any accused person, bringing public shame and significant expense and trouble. A prosecutor cannot bring charges lightly. But Carroll was not cautious in pursuit of fairness but for other reasons. He hated losing, particularly high-profile cases. In each election, he boasted of his high rate of successful convictions, an easy metric to brandish, made possible by cherry-picking cases. Nobody kept track of all the cases that could have been brought but were not. And to the extent some criminal prosecutions, for graft or illegal gambling, might step on the toes of his friends and allies, Carroll had another reason to hold off.

Moreover, Carroll gave short shrift to the other side of the equation. The prosecutor exists to publicly challenge men and women who choose to commit crimes. Carroll's failure to act meant crimes went unpunished. The powerful got their way; the less powerful took their chances. Carroll preferred maintaining a status quo, doing the minimum necessary to keep the peace, punish protesters, and prosecute flag desecrators, but was not interested in seeking out those areas where more serious injustices quietly flourished.

I made clear to my staff—and, through them, to the police — that we were willing to pursue cases where a guilty verdict was not guaranteed. We were not the final decision makers regarding guilt or innocence. Instead, those questions should be finally determined in a public courtroom whenever we believed we had the right person and there was evidence to convict.

## A Cold Case in Kent

The grand jury was an immediate example of the new attitude. None of those indictments were slam dunks, and in the end, we lost most of the cases. But an opportunity to demonstrate there was a new philosophy, even in ordinary cases, came in the case of Eric Haga, an engineer who lived in Kent.

Early in the morning on July 6, 1966, Haga called the Kent police to report he had found his young wife, Judith Ann, and their daughter of seven months, Perri Lynn, strangled at their home. At the inquest, there was testimony that Judith Ann had been having an affair; that Eric suspected Perri Lynn was not his child; and that shortly before the deaths, Eric took out a life insurance policy on his wife. Ultimately, the inquest jury stated the cause was "persons unknown." Carroll declined to prosecute as the evidence was wholly circumstantial.

Eric Haga went on to become a well-known auto racer, regularly driving at Pacific Raceways in Kent and competing at other West Coast venues. Suspicions always lingered, though, and the family, helped by courthouse reporter Virginia Burnside, urged us to reexamine the case. After our own review, we felt there was enough for a jury to find guilt beyond a reasonable doubt. On August 31, 1971, we filed murder charges, and deputies Jim Warme and Lee Yates took the Haga case through two difficult trials and two appeals before guilt was finally confirmed by the supreme court on December 15, 1975.

## The Prosecutor, the Police, and the Community

The real test of the change of culture was whether the prosecutor's office would be perceived differently in the community. Today, in Seattle, there are serious questions of community trust regarding our police department, beginning to be addressed aggressively as I write this by new chief Kathleen O'Toole. In 1970, the same tensions existed in an exacerbated form, particularly between the police and minority communities, and the prosecutor's office was part of the problem. Explaining why requires a bit of backstory.

Over the years, Prosecutor Carroll developed a reputation for letting his conservative ideology and partisan goals influence his charging decisions. Some of the results at the time were troubling but not of long-term consequence: in the late sixties, he pursued student protesters more vigorously than corrupt cops and brought more flag desecration cases than any prosecutor before or since, including charging one hapless woman for wearing a dress decorated with stars and stripes.

But Carroll's ideological leanings caused more enduring trouble with Seattle's black community. He gained a reputation for biased charging decisions that did real and lasting damage to trust between blacks and local law enforcement. Carroll was only one part of that picture; day-to-day conflicts between minorities and police were common and more likely to sour opinions. But as legal head of law enforcement in King County, Carroll played an outsize role, and his actions and lack of action symbolized an indifferent or hostile system.

Carroll never displayed personal racism that I have heard of. Early in his career, Carroll treated blacks as one more ethnic group to placate by making token appointments and attending fund-raisers for black groups. One of Carroll's excellent hires was Charles Z. Smith, who later went on to become judge and then Washington State Supreme Court justice. Smith was a nominal Republican in the fifties when he became a deputy prosecutor but, as he recounts in his oral biography, almost didn't get selected because Carroll already had somebody black. Fortunately, Carroll decided the office could handle one more. In the 1950s, Carroll won awards from the Urban League. But the turmoil of the sixties showed that blacks were not just one more ethnic group.

There have been African Americans in Seattle since the nineteenth century, but until the 1930s, there wasn't a large black population. Seattle's initial racial conflicts concerned other groups: early battles with Native Americans, riots in the 1880s against Chinese immigrants, internment of Japanese Americans during World War II. Washington law never had Jim Crow provisions, though those few blacks who did live here suffered the same informal racism and prejudice common everywhere in the United States.

But World War II and the rise of Boeing increased the city's black population considerably, with both job seekers and soldiers. These newcomers arrived in a city still de facto segregated in housing and employment. Much of Seattle's housing was closed off by racial covenants, prejudiced real estate agents, and redlining, and it was mostly in the Central District that housing could be easily found, transforming that neighborhood into a near ghetto. Blacks also found that jobs were harder to obtain, at least after the war ended. Even in 1970, it took protests, lawsuits, and forceful action by King County executive John Spellman to compel local unions to include blacks in their apprenticeship programs.

Problems with jobs and housing caused frustration, but conflict with police caused outright anger. Minorities regularly complained about police brutality, selective arrests, and general harassment. It did not help that right through the 1960s, the Seattle police force was overwhelmingly white and not particularly enlightened. At the beginning of 1968, the force of nearly a thousand officers had only eight blacks, up from five in 1965. Chief Ramon explained he wanted more but that blacks were simply not interested in joining the force.

# 1965—Larsen Shoots Reese

In this atmosphere, a white officer shooting a black man can crystallize underlying anger. In 1965, two off-duty officers and their wives were attacked in a Central District bar by blacks who were upset because the officers uttered racial slurs. After the fracas wound down, Officer Harold Larsen went outside the bar onto the street corner and shot at a car driving away with some of the assailants, killing Robert Reese. Because it was a police shooting, there was a coroner's inquest, which led to a verdict of "excusable homicide" by the all-white jury. Carroll did prosecute the officer's companion with provoking assault, but did not charge Larsen with fatally shooting Robert Reese. On the other hand, he charged four of the black men involved in the earlier fight with third-degree assault, and all were convicted.

Prosecutor Carroll may have felt he was just being fair in deferring to the inquest and bringing charges against all sides. But the net result—that a white officer suffered no consequences for shooting at a black man- -angered a black population already sensitized to their treatment by the police. A local civil rights leader, Dr. John Adams, decried the "Alabama style" justice being meted out and tied it to a history of black citizens seeking redress for physical and psychological police brutality.

The Robert Reese shooting cast a long shadow. Years later, blacks in Seattle would point to its frustrating legal aftermath as a turning point in their distrust of Seattle's police and prosecutor. Some whites also wanted a better response. The Seattle Human Rights Commission, established under former mayor Gordon Clinton, pushed Mayor Braman and Chief Ramon to set up a community relations squad in the police department. Initially, Ramon asserted there was no need for such a thing, because any complaints could be taken to ranking members of the police department or the

prosecutor. Eventually, though, he caved, and the community relations unit came into being in late 1965. But the CRU proved mostly
ineffective, weakened by departmental indifference to its work.

## Black Radical Protest—White Establishment Pushback

The black community's alienation from the police and prosecutor
after the Reese shooting was exacerbated by the rise of more radical
protests by blacks in the community, leading in turn to strong law
enforcement reaction.

Seattle had the first Black Panther chapter created outside of
Oakland. One of its founders, Aaron Dixon, describes the increasing conflict between the Panthers and the law in his memoir *My
People Are Rising*. A particular sore point noted by Dixon was
Carroll's decision in April 1968 to charge five young men, including Dixon himself, with unlawful assembly for sitting in at Frank-
lin High School and also to charge two juveniles with coercion,
unlawful assembly, and vagrancy for the same event. The juveniles
appeared before Judge Robert Utter (later a Washington Supreme
Court justice), who dismissed the charges against one and found
the other had only violated the vagrancy law. When he heard about
this, Carroll called up Utter and cursed him over the phone, using
a selection of obscenities that Bob Utter never publicly revealed.
When Dan Evans and Slade Gorton spoke at Garfield High School
while campaigning together in August 1968, they were taken aback
by the deep anger the audience directed against Carroll because of
this and earlier incidents.

Matters came to a head in May 1970, when Larry Ward was shot
after bombing Hardcastle Realty. The black community was infuriated by evidence that the police had instigated the crime. The inquest

that followed demonstrated as none before the deficiencies of that archaic system to deal with a controversial shooting. Theoretically, an inquest was convened only to help the county coroner determine the cause of a homicide when there has been a police shooting. During the inquest, a deputy prosecutor questioned witnesses, but the victim was not represented nor did anyone cross-examine. At the time, the inquest jury itself was personally selected by the coroner, a minor elected official not required to have medical or legal credentials. King County's coroner was Leo Sowers, a political ally of Carroll, who, it was rumored, kept a list of prospective jurors in a drawer and simply reused them from one inquest to another.

Although inquests were meant only to find facts, the inquest jury was often asked to make a general determination of whether a crime occurred, and the public tended to accept inquest verdicts as equivalent to findings of guilt or innocence. Almost invariably, juries found a police shooting justified (as happened with the Reese case). During his tenure, Carroll had always accepted those decisions as a final result.

The Larry Ward inquest broke a pattern. Because so many people wanted to watch, it was held at the Seattle Center and quickly became raucous. Lem Howell represented the Ward family. The judge allowed him and other lawyers to interrupt and question witnesses while the crowd itself frequently yelled its disapproval. The result was unexpected: for the first time in over twenty years, the jury voted against the police, by a 3–2 vote, finding Ward died by "criminal means." Carroll chose not to prosecute, citing a lack of evidence, and it was that decision that pushed Howell to later jump into the race for prosecutor.

During my 1970 campaign, I criticized the inquest system and King County's reliance on a coroner instead of a medical examiner. I also promised to further investigate the Ward shooting. Howell drew broader conclusions from Carroll's selective use of his power.

*Members of the Larry Ward inquest jury re-enact the shooting of Ward through a police car window.*

During one of the candidate debates, Howell asked Ed Heavey, "Do you believe a black man can obtain justice in this county?" For Howell, the answer was obvious—no.

## A New Era?

When I came into office, part of restoring trust with Seattle's minorities was hiring deputies who could better represent the community's interests. Chuck Carroll's idea of "diversity" had been like filling a twelve-crayon Crayola box: choose one of each color or ethnic group. He liked to boast his office was a mini–United Nations. But he used his deputies to garner political support from Seattle's organized racial and ethnic communities, not to reach out to them.

My earliest successes were in hiring more women and putting them in responsible positions. It was a good time to make that change. More and more women were attending law school, and we hired some of the best as interns and deputies. In 1971, when I promoted veteran prosecutor Patricia Harber to assistant chief in the criminal division, she was one of only two female deputies. By 1979, one third of the deputy prosecutors were women.

Finding minority lawyers was more difficult; there simply weren't as many in law school or who had recently graduated. To get around the problem, we recruited law students in their first or second year, as interns. Using the Washington State Bar Association's Rule 9 program, we sent them to court for routine matters, which led many to champ at the bit to become deputies after graduation. Judges were often surprised to see a fresh-faced law student before them, but Rule 9 was a great recruiting tool, and we ended up doing a fair job of reversing some of the statistics. As of June 1978, 13 percent of all minority attorneys ever admitted to the state bar had worked for the King County prosecutor, and coincidentally, about 13 percent of our current deputies were members of minority groups, including such outstanding lawyers as Jose Gaitan and Richard Jones.

## Doug Wheeler—Community Contact

I needed to do something more demonstrative than simply hiring deputies from minority communities. I wanted somebody in shop whose full-time job was to mediate between my office and the community. In early 1971, I began talking with black community leaders about how to create this position and who could lead it. We wrangled a federal grant and hired twenty-four-year-old Doug Wheeler. Wheeler had been a counselor at the city jail and was the child of the well-regarded Arthur Wheeler and his wife Eriville, a couple who also raised thirteen foster children at one time or another.

*Doug Wheeler explaining the justice system and my role in it to high school students in his office.*

Among the Wheeler's foster children were a young Jimi Hendrix and his brother Leon. Doug Wheeler recalls watching Jimi Hendrix playing a little wooden guitar while sitting near Lake Washington: "He never went in the water, just played."

Doug Wheeler's own experiences with King County law enforcement showed him its rank underside, as he told me in a recent interview: "Everyone knew it was corrupt. Certain attorneys could guarantee their clients would receive light sentences from judges. Pimps would pay bail bondsmen monthly to insure their women wouldn't be hassled by the police." He was motivated to make a change.

I hired Wheeler to educate the community regarding the prosecutor's office and to educate prosecutors on working with the community. Wheeler met with the Seattle Black Panthers, Save Our Sisters (concerned with rape victims and young prostitutes), the Central Area School Council, and other groups to teach them what a prosecutor could and couldn't do. Wheeler also spoke to prosecutors in the office about communicating with witnesses and defendants. In effect, he mediated between two suspicious communities. I wanted to make sure Doug Wheeler was not seen as a token, so I put him in an office next to mine and gave him free access. This showed the staff he was to be taken seriously, but even better, when people came in from the community, they saw him sitting just outside the door to "the man." Access helped, but what Wheeler did with the access was key.

For one thing, Doug worked one on one. Nearly half of his time was spent handling individuals' problems with the Seattle police or particular prosecutors. Some deputies criticized Wheeler for taking on particular cases, feeling the issues were trivial or a waste of time. But Wheeler responded convincingly that to build trust with the community, he needed to be seen as an actual problem solver. Each person he helped in the relatively small black community of Seattle could pass the word on to others that there was someone to talk to at the prosecutor's office.

By being a sympathetic presence in the office for people who felt they had not been heard, Wheeler made us more effective. Witnesses who might just hang up on a deputy would listen to his voice on the line. And his one-on-one work did not stop him from being a public presence; once he wrote a short play on the dangers of drugs and performed it before high school audiences with background music.

Wheeler had some dramatic moments. I sent him out to handle a confrontation between the Black Panthers and the police outside a sandwich shop near Garfield High School. The shop was known for delivering packets of drugs inside your sandwich, the exact drug depending on the sandwich ordered. The Panthers had no love for drug dealers near schools. Their tactic for shutting the place down was to stand across the street, fifteen of them, all with rifles pointed into the air. That kind of scene attracts attention, and it wasn't long before the Seattle police were lined up on the other side of the street with their own guns in holsters.

Wheeler went there alone and explained to a skeptical police officer first, who he was, and second, that unless the Panthers actually pointed the rifles at someone or otherwise used them in a threatening manner, they weren't committing a crime. Then he walked across the street and told the Panthers to keep their guns pointed in the air and not anywhere else.

Wheeler lasted several years. His own assessment is he changed some attitudes on the street and some in the office. He mentioned a deputy prosecutor who had no real patience for him when he arrived and was a fan when he left. He did not claim the prosecutor's office was particularly loved by the black community but that in the seventies, it at least earned the right to be listened to, a change from previous years when it had lost the benefit of the doubt.

## Equal Justice

The 1965 Robert Reese shooting and the 1970 Larry Ward shooting bracketed years of violence; both outrages committed by radicals and brutalities committed by the police poisoned the mutual atmosphere. Fundamental to the black communities' distrust of the prosecutor's office was the suspicion the prosecutor would always protect the police in a collision with blacks, regardless of circumstances. In my eight years, I had to build an effective relationship with the county's police departments, while still making clear I was beholden neither to the police nor their special protectors and would take citizen complaints about their behavior seriously.

By convening a grand jury that indicted numerous officers, I had already demonstrated the police were not untouchable. Dave

Boerner's charging the eavesdropping Renton cops was another example that police misbehavior would not be ignored. But the roots of minority distrust went deep, and my being tough with the police in some very public situations was not enough to satisfy community leaders.

I tried to address part of this concern by asking the 1971 grand jury to take another look at the Larry Ward case. Witnesses confirmed Larry Ward was persuaded to place a firebomb at Hardcastle Realty by a police informant who had been released on bail and who manufactured the crime to ensure favorable treatment at an upcoming sentencing. But witnesses were conflicted on what happened after Ward placed the bomb at the door and whether the police shouted a warning before opening fire or had reason to gun Ward down as he took off running.

The grand jury chose not to bring an indictment. Unfortunately, the grand jury report was sealed, so the public never saw the grand jury's work or my role in bringing the Ward matter to them.

## Elmore Shoots Black

Ultimately, my office was judged by its decisions in difficult cases. And the most difficult cases came when the police shot somebody and I had to decide whether to charge a police officer. My first opportunity came early. On March 21, 1971, a white police officer named Robert Elmore got into a car chase with a black man, Leslie Allen Black. At the end of the chase, Black abandoned his car and ran, and Elmore shot him down.

John Spellman and I wanted to avoid another Larry Ward fiasco, so we put in place new rules for the Elmore inquest. Fortunately, the post of coroner had been abolished by the new King County charter, so jurors would be picked from a normal jury pool, not

Leo Sowers's bottom drawer. We allowed time for attorneys representing both the victim's family and the officer to appear and ask questions, and broadened the scope so the jury could make specific factual findings and not just file general verdicts.

The inquest itself proceeded more smoothly, but the results were still confusing. On April 17, the inquest found Elmore had shot Black to effect an arrest but that the shooting was contrary to department guidelines and not actually necessary to make the arrest. They also found the officer did not have probable cause to believe he was in danger of injury. The 5–1 vote on the last point marked a rare occasion where an inquest jury simply failed to believe a police officer, for Elmore had testified he thought Black had a gun.

The ball was now in my court—to charge Elmore or not—at a particularly bad time. It was the first week of grand jury sessions. Two weeks earlier, Chief Tielsch had punished Eugene Corr for cooperating with the grand jury staff, and there'd been some back and forth in the press. Charging Elmore with a crime would further alienate the police department, whose cooperation I needed.

While my staff and I were pondering, a delegation of ten black radicals invaded the offices of acting mayor Charles M. Carroll and County Executive John Spellman, and demanded blacks serve on all trial juries where blacks were defendants and that the black community help select inquest judges. Spellman threw them out, stating he would decide who the judge was.

In the end, I determined the inquest findings matched up with the evidence, which showed Elmore shot a man fleeing after a high-speed chase without good reason to think the man posed a danger. That was a criminal act under the law, and accordingly, on April 23, we charged Elmore with manslaughter. It was the first time in anybody's memory a prosecutor indicted an officer for shooting a civilian.

For this, I earned some praise from liberal quarters. The Central Area Community Council sent me a statement saying:

> Many people had come to think that the law interpreted and applied in a discriminatory fashion in Seattle and they had reason to think so. You have served notice that the laws will apply equally to all, policeman as well as private citizen. You have confirmed public confidence in your office and in law enforcement in King County.

But most of the public disliked the charges. The police guild, many private citizens, and most eloquently, Elmore's wife, all wrote me letters making the same points: Elmore was a good officer, Black was a criminal (evidence emerged he had been driving a stolen car that night), Elmore had good reason to think Black was armed, and there was nothing wrong in shooting at a fleeing felon. I received so much mail I developed a form-letter response—that equal justice required equal treatment of all those committing homicide.

The trial took place in November 1971, conducted by Chief Criminal Deputy Dave Boerner. Defending Elmore were Neal Shulman, who had been chief criminal deputy under Carroll before resigning, and Joel Rindal. The all-white jury took less than an hour to reach their verdict: not guilty. Elmore immediately returned to patrol duties.

And thus, the results were mixed. The black community may have been heartened that a prosecutor took seriously the idea that the police should be judged by the same law as anybody else. On the other hand, the quick verdict of the jury showed the legal system as a whole was not necessarily similarly inclined.

## 1975—Earlywine Shoots Hebert

I did not face another high-profile police-shooting decision until February 1975. SPD officer Allen Earlywine and his partner heard about a Woodinville robbery committed by five black men. They staked out the Mercer Island bridge, a logical place to intercept Woodinville robbers returning to Seattle. The officers recognized a car from a previous robbery, signaled it to pull over, and ordered the driver, Joseph Hebert, to get out. Hebert got out, ran, and was shot.

The shooting was widely publicized, and the inquest results were widely anticipated. Unfortunately, as in the Elmore case, the results were confusing. Earlywine testified he fired in self-defense, after Hebert wheeled on him holding what Earlywine thought was a gun but which proved to be a knife. Hebert's family attorney tried to show the story was a lie. The inquest jury, which included two black jurors and was conducted by a black judge, found by a 5–1 vote the homicide was not justifiable. But by a 4–2 vote, they also found the officer had been in reasonable fear for his life.

From a legal standpoint, my decision whether or not to prosecute was more difficult than in the Black-Elmore case. The touchstone of a case against Earlywine would be whether he acted in reasonable self-defense. The jury verdict indicated some would believe he had. After a two-day review of the testimony, we decided not to file.

The black community's negative reaction was fierce and swift. It did not help that newly appointed chief Robert Hanson held a press conference the next day to reveal Hebert's long criminal record and that property from the Woodinville robbery had been found in his abandoned car. Hanson was rightly condemned for attacking a dead man and raising points irrelevant to whether Earlywine acted legally in shooting him.

My decision had been based on objective legal factors, but this cut no ice with critics. The ACLU was one of the more restrained:

We suggest that public questioning of your lack of objectivity reflects an accurate perception that the office of prosecutor cannot be objective in these matters. That is not a question of your personal integrity but of the institutional relationship between the police and the prosecutor. The prosecutor has a conflict of interest in dealing with potential police criminal conduct (because the two work so closely together).

Lem Howell was a little less kind, directly accusing me of failing to charge in order to protect my political future. I also had the dubious privilege of being interviewed by Calvin Trillin, who arrived to report to his *New Yorker* audience on the Hebert shooting. His depiction of my role was neither favorable nor fair, implying my decision not to charge Earlywine was related to my political advocacy for sentencing reform. But Trillin's summary of the black community's feelings rang true: "A white policeman confronted by a black man may leave a few of the alternatives to shooting unexplored. Chief Hanson tried to make the black people of Seattle see Joe Hebert as a criminal, but they insisted on seeing him as a black man."

After I left office in 1981, my successor, Norm Maleng, charged a prison guard with manslaughter after a prisoner was choked to death, despite an inquest finding the death was justified. The jury acquitted the guard. Not long after the legislature amended the law in this area to provide that a "peace officer shall not be held criminally liable for using deadly force without malice and with a good faith belief that such act is justifiable." Since then, in the words of Prosecutor Dan Satterberg, "This almost perfect defense to a mistaken use of force has kept police officers out of court as defendants."

Reese's death in 1965, Ward's in 1970, and the shootings by Elmore and Earlywine may seem dated now. But each was remembered for a time, and the memories were passed on to new generations in the form of mistrust of police. I think the other work I was doing in the office counterbalanced the anger caused by particular decisions on particular shootings, but it only takes one difficult decision to lose a lot of the community's trust.

## Leaving

My part of the story ends here. Early in 1978, I announced I would not run for a third term as King County prosecuting attorney. I wanted either to join a law firm and make more money for my growing family or reach for some higher office—for example, replacing the ever more unpopular Governor Dixy Ray. And I did not want to become another Carroll, a man who outlived his usefulness in office. Hoping to clear the field, I announced at the same time that my highly talented chief civil deputy, Norm Maleng, would be a distinguished successor. Maleng won in 1978 and went on, in his own storied career, to be reelected numerous times as prosecutor but to lose at attempts for higher office.

After leaving office, I eventually decided against another campaign. John Spellman had earned the shot against Ray, and he prevailed in his second run for governor. I interviewed with several large law firms and accepted an offer to head up municipal finance at Perkins Coie, then managed by Tom Alberg. After that, I had a wonderful ten years at Burlington Northern, helping Dick Bressler and team assemble a transportation and resources conglomerate, only to take it all apart because the market still thought we were only a railroad. In the end, we made the original Burlington Northern shareholders very happy.

My final political fling was an unsuccessful effort to win the Republican primary for the US Senate in 1998. I lost badly to the feisty and very conservative Representative Linda Smith, who in turn was overwhelmed by Senator Patty Murray, who has been there ever since.

Looking back on my eight years as prosecutor, I am proud of the substantive accomplishments. Those were the years when King County successfully battled Major League Baseball in court to secure a team and build its first major sports stadium, the subsequently imploded Kingdome. Gene Anderson was recruited to create a fraud division that cracked down on consumer rackets and crooked judges. At one point, we staked out the toll booths on the Evergreen Point bridge over Lake Washington, complete with cameras hidden in trees, to film toll takers pocketing change. My office spearheaded reforms to King County's antiquated juvenile court system and changes to state law on juvenile justice. We also took the lead in defending recently enacted environmental laws, in particular the Shoreline Management Act, in the teeth of fierce opposition from Weyerhaeuser and other timber companies. All those are other stories, but the best things that happened during those eight years, were that I married my wife, Cynthia, and our two daughters were born.

The most important change took place apart from these events, large and small: the change in the culture of the prosecuting attorney's office. In a word, it became professional, not political. I was elected to reform the office. And I believe I was successful.

# DEATH OF A WOOD-CARVER

★ ★ ★ ★ ★ ★ ★ ★ ★ ★ ★ ★

In the last few years, including my time spent working on this book in the spring of 2015, the Seattle Police Department has been troubled. There have been court cases, federal investigations, and a revolving door for police chiefs. And the principal cause was a police shooting.

On August 30, 2010, John T. Williams, a homeless Native American wood-carver, was walking on a downtown street, holding the three-inch knife he used to whittle. Officer Ian Birk pulled up near him, got out of his car, told Williams to drop the knife, and, four seconds later, shot and killed him. The inquest took place the following January and included two weeks of evidence, including Birk's statement he feared for his life. As usual, the public treated the inquest as if it were a trial. And, again, the inquest jury was divided.

Regarding the crucial questions of whether Birk faced an imminent threat or had provided Williams sufficient time to disarm, the jury split three ways: on each question, four said no, three said "unknown," and one said yes. Regarding the other important issue, whether Birk believed he was in danger, the jury split right down the middle: four yes, four no. Before and after the inquest, King County's current prosecuting attorney, Dan Satterberg, reviewed

1,200 emails and many letters concerning the case. He was unsuccessful in an attempt to meet with the victim's family but did meet with members of the Native American community. In the end, he decided not to charge Birk, citing the law referenced above that protects police officers from criminal charges, if they acted in good faith and without malice. (Birk resigned within hours of that decision, following a departmental review finding the shooting unjustified.) Satterberg later said it was one of his hardest decisions in office and spoke of the need "to bridge the deep divide of mistrust" between the community and the police department.

The shooting of Williams and the decision not to prosecute Birk set in motion a series of events. The ACLU and numerous other organizations were not willing to let Satterberg's decision be the last word. They had documented examples of police violence going back to 2009, and the Williams shooting was not just a last straw but a cattle prod. Jumping past layers of municipal and local government, these groups asked the US Department of Justice to investigate and also brought a class action suit in federal court.

The DOJ launched its investigation on March 31, 2011, six weeks after the decision not to charge Birk. The result of the investigation appeared in December 2011 and shocked the city, particularly city hall. Assistant Attorney General Thomas Perez, head of the civil rights division, concluded officers engaged in a "pattern and practice" of excessive force. Perez said the investigation also uncovered troubling evidence of biased policing but lacked the data to find a pattern. He also said the department's practices to assure accountability and public trust were "broken" and that the only sure fix would be through court-ordered long-term reform with an outside special monitor to oversee it. It was a proposal not since WWII—direct federal intervention into the Seattle Police Department.

Mayor Mike McGinn and Chief John Diaz resisted the report's conclusion, with the chief insisting that the department was not "broken" and that needed reforms could be made internally. In the end, neither mayor nor chief could withstand pressure from the public and an unsympathetic city council. The litigation and investigation finally resulted in a settlement agreement between the city and the DOJ in August 2012.

SPD leadership during this period underwent the same rapid turnover that characterized it in 1969 and 1970. From 2009 to 2014, the city has had four police chiefs. John Diaz, Jim Pugel, and Harry Bailey held the position before new mayor Ed Murray put in place Chief Kathleen O'Toole after a national search. O'Toole came to office with wide acclaim and a reputation for being a self-confident leader who could bring some stability to the department.

## Then and Now

As someone once said, history doesn't repeat itself, but it does rhyme. The problems the Seattle Police Department faces today are not the same as the payoff and corruption scandals of the sixties and seventies. But there are some familiar chords.

The payoff system was created by a police department so insular and self-regarding that ranking staff believed a valid purpose of law enforcement was to generate profits for police. Much of the top brass were simply greedy. But their greed was facilitated by the dysfunctional culture of the rank and file, the product of years of low pay, overwork, and dangerous working conditions that built up a resentful police force alienated from the community it served and unwilling to put public service ahead of loyalty to fellow officers. It took brave reformers who were willing to buck their friends and colleagues to end the corruption.

No one has accused Seattle's current police force of personal corruption or graft. The federal and county criminal trials of 1970 to 1974 put a stake through the heart of that vampire. The current SPD is a professional outfit that puts a higher value on public service than private profit. The recent allegations of brutality or misjudgment do not indicate a police department seeking to profit from its position. So there has been permanent change. But the current controversies demonstrate a department that is still alienated from the community, still inclined to a secretive and self-protective crouch when criticized, and still disinclined to self-reform.

In 1970 and 1971, the SPD resisted investigation, and idealistic officers like Gustin, Corr, Fuller, Jessup, and Price suffered for speaking out. In 2010, as the Williams inquest was about to begin, individual members of the department, speaking in their guild newsletter, defended the actions of Officer Birk against the "lynch mob," deplored the socialism inherent in requiring diversity training, and indicated that civilian review boards were not to be feared as their decisions could always be ignored. (These characterizations are taken from reporters describing the contents of articles in the police guild newsletter, the *Guardian*, in the last half of 2010, prior to the Williams inquest. Unfortunately, I was not able to read the articles themselves, as they are not available for viewing by anyone who is not a member of the police department—a reflection in itself of a certain insularity.) In their opposition to the federal court order, over one hundred officers filed their own lawsuit to prevent new rules on police use of force. The department itself fought against public release of dashboard videos, only losing in the supreme court after protracted litigation.

I think what can be taken away from these episodes, forty years apart, is that reform of the police department, like reform of the prosecutor's office or city hall, works best when it is not seen as ridding the department of a few bad apples but when the system itself and the mindset of the people involved in the system are changed. There are steps in that direction now, most significantly those taken by former King County sheriff Sue Rahr, who now heads the state police academy. Her stated goal is to change the philosophy of the police from a Warrior Model, in which a cop in a problem situation attempts to immediately control the behavior of everybody around him—for example, by forcing people to their knees—to the Guardian Model, where the goal is to defuse violence and listen to the actual concerns of the people who are upset. I agree with Sue Rahr. It is this kind of reasoned, measured response to persistent social problems that is the hallmark of a good law enforcement system. Making this type of cultural change is crucial to forestalling future scandals and turmoil for the department. Hopefully, Rahr will be helped by city and county elected officials, such as Tim Burgess, now the city council president, who was himself a Seattle police officer for eight years and has recently been a strong proponent of reform.

Standing beside and supporting these reform efforts is a King County prosecutor's office that has remained professional and become highly respected. Although it remains officially a partisan office, the current occupant, Dan Satterberg, and his predecessor, Norm Maleng, have steered a resolutely nonpartisan course, even during those years when Maleng sought higher office.

Satterberg's initiatives have included working with Doug Wheeler on the 180 Program, which provides juvenile criminals with real alternatives to continuing with crime. The shooting of John Williams and the contested aftermath of the inquest strained Satterberg's relationship with the community, particularly the minority community, but it did not break it. By his actions before and since, Satterberg has built up a balance of trust in the community's accounts. Measuring trust is inherently difficult, but a telling sign is that in a city deeply Democratic, with a vibrant and outspoken leftist constituency, neither Maleng nor

Satterberg, both nominal Republicans, have ever faced a serious electoral challenge.

## As for Seattle's Politicians

Seattle's city hall and county courthouse had their own problems with real and perceived corruption in the fifties and sixties; the grand jury indictments in 1971 included a city councilmember, a county licensing director, and, of course, the former King County prosecuting attorney. But since then, Seattle's political culture has also changed in city hall. One of the few significant subsequent scandals dates to the early 2000s, when Frank Colacurcio, a Seattle icon of criminality even into his eighth decade, steered some illegal campaign funds to city councilmembers to influence a vote on a parking rezone benefiting his strip club north of Lake City. Former governor Al Rosellini, then in his ninth decade, got into his own sort of trouble by making introductions between father and son Colacurcio and the pliable councilmembers. Governor Rosellini never could see the harm in helping friends in need.

But if this was a political fix, it was characterized by such ineptitude that one wonders if the "bought" councilmembers really knew what they were doing. They showed up at a committee meeting for a vote where they normally would not have appeared, attracting press attention that exposed the campaign contributions and their dubious provenance. The long-lasting Frank Colacurcio bought himself renewed attention, local charges for bribery (subsequently dismissed), and eventually an FBI investigation into a variety of crimes, including cold case murders, that chased him until his death in 2010 at the age of ninety-three. In days long ago, the press might have been more forgiving, public attention more fleeting and more forgiving, and prosecutions less likely.

On the city council, turnover slowed to a standstill between 2000 and 2009, and the critiques of this stasis reminded me of the criticisms of the council that led to the creation of CHECC in 1967. However, this time there was no bipartisan reform effort, which is understandable as there have been no Republicans active in city government since the days of Paul Kraabel. Things perked up in 2013 with the defeat of longtime incumbent Richard Conlin by avowed socialist Kshama Sawant. Now that we have chosen election by district, who knows where the city council will end up, but there's no sign the city will ever return to a system as stagnant and institutionally corrupt as was true in the fifties and sixties.

## Ferguson and Seattle and a Story That Never Ends

Even as I find signs of progress, the events of Ferguson, Missouri, and police shootings in other cities fill the news and overtake my story. The shooting in the Saint Louis suburb and its aftermath have spurred a national conversation, louder than in many a year, on the role and tactics of police departments and prosecutors, and on the fairness of the justice system as a whole. I hope this conversation will be continuing when this book is published. For myself, I can speak only from a perch far removed from the practical concerns of actually being part of the justice system. But I still think the experience of the past has a lesson to teach.

Public trust in the justice system is most robust where the public understands how the system works and where citizens know they can rely on those they elect to make it work fairly. The fundamental problem at the end of Carroll's tenure as prosecutor was that he lost the trust of our community, a trust that he would apply the same standards of justice to politicians and police officers as he would to an ordinary citizen. A prosecutor is supposed to enact justice. Too often, Carroll's actions appeared designed only to further his personal ambition and political beliefs. When large numbers of citizens no longer believe the officers of their government, however human, are motivated by justice but instead by personal gain or prejudice, then the justice system as a whole has lost its way. Police and prosecutors become perceived simply as an oppressive force, operating on their own agendas.

Broken trust is difficult to repair. For members of a community who have long felt aggrieved by the justice system, each new incident, whatever its individual circumstances, is measured against a history of problems. Any protester marching today, as I write this, thinks not just of the details of a shooting on the streets of Ferguson, Missouri, but of shootings in other places and other times. The responsible authorities of every city in the United States must operate with a sense of that history.

My goal as prosecutor was never to set the office against any part of the community but instead to find ways to draw citizens into the common project of doing justice. I am immensely proud of the work of my successors, Maleng and Satterberg, to continue this model and to extend and amplify the work. My belief is that the King County prosecutor's office has continued to be trusted by the county's citizens. The events of Ferguson demonstrate the consequences when that trust is lost, by prosecutors, police, or both.

Police officers and prosecutors will always be human and will always make human mistakes. Police officers, in particular, have the unenviable task of sometimes making split-second decisions where the consequences of getting the decision wrong could be their lives or somebody else's. But trust is won when members of the justice system accept scrutiny for their actions and mistakes, even those made in good faith, and demonstrate a willingness to make the changes needed to better perform their mission.

The indictments brought by Stan Pitkin and myself were the first time the Seattle Police Department faced serious sustained scrutiny of its practices. It emerged better for the ordeal, a department subsequently free from graft and corruption. The department shows every sign that the recent federal court monitoring will also improve its procedures around the use of force, hopefully reducing the chances of future shootings that leave the community divided.

But it is long past the time that reform comes only by pressure from outside. Every prosecutor's office, police department, court official, or municipal officeholder should welcome criticism and scrutiny, not resist it. It is easy, too easy, for members of a bureaucracy to keep doing the same things that have worked tolerably well in the past. But every contested police shooting, community protest, or incident of municipal corruption should be a signal to those who serve the public that they need to reexamine their own methods. And in doing so, they need to keep in mind the history of their offices and the memories of the citizens they serve. As Dan Satterberg, discussing the recent upheavals, told me: "The challenge in the Ferguson/Staten Island era is to establish law enforcement legitimacy in *every* neighborhood. When protestors speak Truth to Power, Power has to sit and listen."

It's a common experience for a Seattleite to walk down a street where there is a hole in the ground and a new building rising and wonder what used to be there without really being able to remember. The same is true for our political history. The ways of thinking that led to the creation of Seattle's Tolerance Policy would seem strange now. Today, if there are activities living in a legal gray world—for example, retail marijuana that coexists uneasily with federal drug laws—the problems of enforcement and tolerance are worked out in public, and the lines made clear. The city no longer tolerates hypocrisy simply for the financial gain or shrugs at graft that is too entrenched to fix.

But some things never change. Governments that become inbred, that resist change or scrutiny or criticism, always lose their way, whatever the good faith of those inside. I was a reformer once in a time of miraculous, wonderful and positive change. But the need for reform never ends. My hope for Seattle is that its leaders will continue to challenge dysfunction and injustice whenever and wherever it is found in our fair city.

# ACKNOWLEDGMENTS

★ ★ ★ ★ ★ ★ ★ ★ ★ ★ ★ ★

The book you are holding would not have been possible without the assistance of Glenn MacGilvra, my researcher and my collaborator on the writing of much of the Seattle history herein. He took over and completed the work of earlier assistants Nate Weston and Helene Smart. I am grateful to all of them and to Joanna Crocker for finding Glenn. And I am indebted to our editor at Sasquatch, Hannah Elnan, for her crucial help in organizing and improving the content.

Many of my former colleagues and political friends inspired me to write this book. Prominent among them are Judge Robin Hunt, former US attorneys Mike and John McKay, former prosecutor's office leaders Dave Boerner and John Keegan, and my old friends and political colleagues Tom Alberg and Bruce Chapman. Former collaborators in the HYRC, Ripon Society, CHECC, Action for Washington, and many political campaigns are also part of the story and fondly remembered.

The leadership that took over in January 1971 was remarkable in many ways, and I'm sorry there isn't room here to discuss our reforms over the following eight years. I owe a great deal to chief deputies Dave Boerner, Norm Maleng, and Gene Anderson, as well as Chief of Staff Richard Allison. One characteristic that seems amazing today is that we were all the same age, having graduated from college in or around 1960.

An even stronger regret is that longtime King County prosecutor Norm Maleng is no longer here to read this. Norm is an important part of a larger story that has played out in King County and Washington State over the past fifty years. Washington attorneys general Slade Gorton, Ken Eikenberry, Christine Gregoire, and Rob McKenna; US attorneys Gene Anderson, both McKays, and Jenny Durkan; and the three King County prosecutors you read about here have all built upon the Justice Model we worked to create after the 1970 election. We are of different political persuasions, but each has demonstrated complete independence of party or politics in making difficult decisions. This is the way, the only way, our justice system can be maintained and strengthened when under pressure and in difficult times.

# A NOTE ON SOURCES

★ ★ ★ ★ ★ ★ ★ ★ ★ ★ ★ ★

In addition to my own memories and collected papers, I have several other sources for this book:

**INTERVIEWS:** Over the course of the last five years, my associates and I have interviewed numerous people from politics and the press, including Governor Evans, Mayor Uhlman, the late Justice Utter, the late Lou Guzzo of the *P-I*, journalists Rick Anderson and Ross Anderson, and members of the 1970 campaign. We have received important help from several of the deputy prosecutors in my office and in Charles O. Carroll's.

**ARCHIVAL RESEARCH:** The University of Washington Special Collections has many collections of personal papers of prominent individuals. The most important set of papers for this book was my own, the Christopher Bayley collection, which includes materials from my days as a prosecutor as well as other materials. Also significant were papers left by former mayor Dorm Braman and those of Dean Leffler.

Other archives consulted include the Seattle Municipal Archives at Seattle City Hall, King County Archives, and the Seattle Room of the Seattle Public Library's Central Library.

214 | A NOTE ON SOURCES

Of particular interest were records kept by the King County Prosecuting Attorney's Office, though unfortunately the grand jury records themselves are still sealed.

**ARCHIVAL NEWSPAPERS:** Of invaluable assistance was the fact that most of the *Seattle Times* is searchable online, through collaboration with the Seattle Public Library. This provides the ability to quickly find the date of a particular event, along with a description, making all the rest of the work easier. Articles in the *P-I* were also of vital interest, though confined to microfiche.

**MUSEUM OF HISTORY AND INDUSTRY (MOHAI):** The archives at MOHAI included numerous excellent photos.

**PREVIOUSLY PUBLISHED BOOKS AND ARTICLES:** Important sources of information were previous articles and books that touch on the subjects involved. Two stand out among the rest: *On the Take* by William Chambliss and *Seattle Vice* by Rick Anderson. Also significant were accounts of Seattle's early history: *Skid Road* by Murray Morgan and *Sons of the Profits* by William Speidel. Additional sources include a story by Ross Anderson in *Seattle Metropolitan* magazine, "Seattle Confidential," and numerous articles from *Seattle* magazine, which had a brief but memorable run of investigative journalism in Seattle from 1964 to 1970. A full list of books consulted is provided in the bibliography.

**SEATTLE METROPOLITAN POLICE MUSEUM:** Located in Pioneer Square is a labor of love, a privately supported museum dedicated to the Seattle Police Department. The numerous exhibits were a valuable resource on the early history of the department.

**HISTORY LINK:** We are fortunate in Washington to have available a free online source of local history: www.historylink.org. Its numerous articles cover a wide range of incidents, events, and topics, including numerous personal accounts.

**LEGACY WASHINGTON:** At this website, www.sos.wa.gov/legacy, are free full-length biographies of some of Washington's public figures. They include oral histories that provide the invaluable gift of hearing people tell their own stories. As a whole, the Legacy Project is a wonderful resource for Washington State history.

# BIBLIOGRAPHY

★ ★ ★ ★ ★ ★ ★ ★ ★ ★ ★ ★

## Books

Anderson, Rick. *Seattle Vice: Strippers, Prostitution, Dirty Money, and Crooked Cops in the Emerald City.* Seattle: Sasquatch Books, 2010.

Chambliss, William J. *On the Take: From Petty Crooks to Presidents.* Bloomington: Indiana University Press, 1978.

Crowley, Walt. *Rites of Passage: A Memoir of the Sixties in Seattle.* Seattle: University of Washington Press, 1997.

Dixon, Aaron. *My People Are Rising: Memoir of a Black Panther Party Captain.* Chicago: Haymarket Books, 2012.

Haarsager, Sandra. *Bertha Knight Landes of Seattle: Big-City Mayor.* Norman: University of Oklahoma Press, 1994.

Hughes, John C. *John Spellman: Politics Never Broke His Heart.* Olympia: Washington State Legacy Project, 2013.

Jones, Nard. *Seattle.* Garden City, NY: Doubleday, 1972.

Morgan, Murray. *Skid Road: An Informal Portrait of Seattle.* Seattle: University of Washington Press, 1982.

Potts, Ralph Bushnell. *Seattle Heritage.* Seattle: Superior Publishing, 1955.

Sale, Roger. *Seattle: Past to Present*. Seattle: University of
Washington Press, 1978.

Speidel, William. *Sons of the Profits; or, There's No Business Like
Grow Business: The Seattle Story, 1851–1901*. Kansas City, MO:
Nettle Creek Printing, 1997.

Watson, Emmett. *Digressions of a Native Son*. Seattle: Pacific
Institute, 1982.

## Articles

Anderson, Ross. "Seattle Confidential." *Seattle Metropolitan*.
February 2007, 86–92.

LeSourd, Peter. "The Transformation of Seattle: CHECC's Role."
Unpublished article, 2008.

Trillin, Calvin. "U.S. Journal: Seattle; Causes and Circumstances."
*New Yorker*. June 2, 1975, 101–6.

# INDEX

★ ★ ★ ★ ★ ★ ★ ★ ★ ★ ★

Note: Photographs are indicated
by *italics*.

# ABOUT THE
# AUTHOR

★ ★ ★ ★ ★ ★ ★ ★ ★ ★ ★ ★

**CHRISTOPHER T. BAYLEY** is a third-generation Seattleite, both of whose grandfathers moved here from back east in the late nineteenth century. He attended Seattle Public Schools followed by college and law school at Harvard University. He has been a lawyer, politician, and business executive since returning to Seattle in 1966. Bayley served in the US Navy aboard USS *Abbot* (DD-629) in the Atlantic fleet and retired as a reserve captain in 1983. This book focuses on his political career in the late 1960s, culminating in his election as King County prosecuting attorney in 1970. Bayley founded Stewardship Partners in 1999 and currently consults on environmental, legal, and business issues.